Everybody enjoys a secret. Surely that is one reason
wh͟.......................................͟ve
c
f
c
b
b
t
c
c
n
a

Critics' Corner:

". . . a stimulating must for the intermediate cryptographer. . . . Gardner covers easy transposition and substitution ciphers and harder polyalphabetic ones, as well as grilles (grids), various kinds of invisible writing and 'bizarre methods' of sending codes, with examples, anecdotes, a little theory, and instructions on breaking and composing ciphers. He explains even the more difficult examples with admirable clarity, alludes to literature (frequently), history, math and science (including the genetic code) with fingertip control, ends with a discussion of radio codes prepared for interplanetary communication, and appends an excellent annotated bibliography. *—The Kirkus Reviews* (starred review)

"Most children are intrigued by the idea of secret messages and, in this well-written and comprehensive book, they'll find a wealth of suggestions on *sub rosa* communications." *—Publishers Weekly*

"A book that should delight the puzzle fan. . . ."
—Bulletin of the Center for Children's Books, University of Chicago

Also recommended by: Library Journal.

About the Author:

MARTIN GARDNER was born in Tulsa, Oklahoma, and graduated from the University of Chicago. The author of the monthly column "Mathematical Games" in *Scientific American,* he has written several books for adults, including six collections of Mathematical Puzzles and Diversions from his magazine column. His books for young people include *Perplexing Puzzles and Tantalizing Teasers* and *Space Puzzles: Curious Questions and Answers About the Solar System,* both of which are in Archway Paperback editions. Mr. Gardner and his wife and two sons make their home in Hastings-on-Hudson, New York.

Martin Gardner

CODES, CIPHERS AND SECRET WRITING

AN ARCHWAY PAPERBACK
POCKET BOOKS · NEW YORK

For

OSVVZ   ZYTZC   KJLQZ

CODES, CIPHERS AND SECRET WRITING

Simon and Schuster edition published 1972

Archway Paperback edition published January, 1974

L

Published by
POCKET BOOKS, a division of Simon & Schuster, Inc.,
630 Fifth Avenue, New York, N.Y.

Archway Paperback editions are distributed in the U.S.
by Simon & Schuster, Inc., 630 Fifth Avenue, New
York, N.Y. 10020, and in Canada by Simon & Schuster
of Canada, Ltd., Richmond Hill, Ontario, Canada.

Standard Book Number: 671-29585-3.
Library of Congress Catalog Card Number: 72-82218.
This Archway Paperback edition is published by arrange-
ment with Simon & Schuster, Inc. Text copyright, ©, 1972,
by Martin Gardner. All rights reserved. This book, or por-
tions thereof, may not be reproduced by any means without
permission of the original publisher: Simon and Schuster,
630 Fifth Avenue, New York, N.Y. 10020.
Printed in the U.S.A.

Contents

Introduction

Cryptography, the writing and deciphering of messages in secret code, and other forms of secret writing have always played, and still play today, vital roles in the history of every nation. It is necessary in this crazy world of ours for governments and spies to send special information in secret ciphers. It is just as necessary for every major nation to have a staff of expert cryptanalysts who work day and night, with electronic computers at their elbows, to crack the codes used by other countries. The history of cryptanalysis (so marvelously told by David Kahn in his comprehensive book *The Codebreakers*) is a fascinating one, filled with dramatic incidents in which the fates of empires and political leaders hinged on the success or failure of a small group of specialists in this ancient, curious kind of puzzle solving.

I say "small" because in earlier centuries such work was often done by only a few cryptanalysts, sometimes only by one man. Today, codebreaking is a vast and rapidly growing profession. No one knows exactly how many people are now engaged in codebreaking for the United States, but they certainly number in the tens of thousands and cost us more than a billion dollars a year. During World War II, 30,000 persons in Great Britain alone were assigned to such work. It is probably our government's most reliable method of gathering intelligence.

The United States Navy's great victory at Midway Island in 1942 was a direct consequence of our having learned the secret of Japan's PURPLE machine code, a remarkable feat of codebreaking that will be described in Chapter 5. In the same war Germany's 1943 U-boat victories against Allied shipping were the result of Germany having broken the British merchant ship code. The tide did not turn until American and British cryptanalysts solved the cipher that was being used by German submarines.

The most sensational solution of a single coded message in recent history occurred during World War I. In 1917 Arthur Zimmermann, the German foreign minister, sent a cable to Mexico, using a diplomatic code called 0075. It announced Germany's plan to begin unrestricted submarine warfare. If America entered the war, the cable continued, Germany promised to give Mexico the states of Arizona, Texas and New Mexico if Mexico would only join in fighting against the United States. The cable was intercepted and the code broken by British intelligence, then passed on to President Woodrow Wilson.

America had been reluctant to enter the war. But news about the Zimmermann telegram so enraged Congress and the public that we declared war on Germany. Had we not done so, it is probable that Germany would have won the war. "Never before or since," writes Kahn, "has so much turned upon the solution of a secret message."

Interest in cryptography is not restricted to governments and professional spies. Everybody enjoys a secret. Surely that is one reason why so many young people like to send and receive coded messages even when there is no special reason for them to be secret. Coded messages are fun to encipher (put in cipher form) and decipher (translate back to the original), and it is even more fun to break a code used by someone else. If you belong to a secret club, you and your friends may want to communicate with one another by one of the methods explained in this book. If you keep a diary, you may wish to protect it from prying eyes by using a code.

Many famous people have written all or parts of their diaries in code. When Franklin Delano Roosevelt was twenty-one, he used a cipher for four entries in a diary he was then keeping. In 1971 these entries were shown for the first time to several cryptographers, who had no trouble breaking the code. It was a simple substitution cipher using numbers for vowels and symbols for consonants. The translations proved to be so tame that one wonders why young Roosevelt bothered to put the entries in code.

If you are clever and diligent, you, too, can learn how to break secret codes. The solving of substitution ciphers is now a popular type of puzzle with enough fans to support a daily "cryptogram" in hundreds of newspapers throughout the country. There is even an American Cryptogram Association which publishes a bimonthly periodical called *The Cryptogram*. (If you are interested, you can write to the treasurer at 604 W. Monroe St., Mexico, Missouri 65265.) Chapter 3 will introduce you to the exciting art of solving cryptograms.

The main purpose of this book, however, is to teach you how to use the most important codes, and other methods of secret communication, that have been invented since ancient times. A selected list of references at the end of the book will provide more reading material about the unusual techniques that have been employed for making ciphers, and for breaking ciphers used by others.

I am indebted to David B. Eisendrath, Jr., for many excellent suggestions which I have followed in Chapter 6, and to David Kahn for writing *The Codebreakers,* my principal source of information.

MARTIN GARDNER

CODES, CIPHERS AND SECRET WRITING

CHAPTER 1

Easy
Transposition
Ciphers

A transposition cipher is one that does not change any letters of the original message. (Cryptographers call the original the "plaintext" but we will simply call it the "message.") It merely rearranges the letters, according to a secret system, so that anyone who knows the system can put the letters back in their proper order and read the message.

The simplest transposition cipher is made by just writing the message backward. AGENT 427 IS ON HIS WAY becomes YAW SIH NO SI 724 TNEGA. If the message happens to be a palindrome—a sentence that reads the same in both directions— the letters will be in exactly the same order when reversed. For example: PULL UP IF I PULL UP, or 'TIS IVAN ON A VISIT. This is not likely to happen, however, with any genuine message.

The main trouble with backward writing is that it is too easy to recognize. If you keep the original word order, but reverse the letters of each word separately, the reversal is a bit harder to spot, but not much. The following transposition ciphers are better and almost as easy to remember and use.

1 · The Rail Fence Cipher

Suppose you wish to encipher this message:

MEET ME TONIGHT

Count the number of letters. If the number is a multiple of 4, well and good. If not, add enough dummy letters at the end to make the number a multiple of 4. In this case there are 13 letters so we add three dummy letters, QXZ, to total 16. Such dummy letters are called "nulls." In a moment we will see why the nulls are added.

Write the message by printing every other letter a trifle lower on the page. The message will look something like a rail fence:

```
M E M T N G T X
 E T E O I H Q Z
```

Copy the top row, then continue by copying the lower row.

Encoding and decoding is simpler and more accurate if you divide the cipher text into groups of four or five letters each, because it is easy to keep that many letters in your head when you write. Besides, this makes the cipher harder to "crack" by the "enemy" because the divisions between the words are not indicated. In this book we will use a 4-group system. That was why three nulls were added in the preceding message. By increasing the number of letters to 16, we make sure that the last group of letters in the cipher text will have four letters like all the other groups.

This is how the final cipher text will appear:

MEMT   NGTX   ETEO   IHQZ

Decoding the message is just as easy as encoding. First divide the cipher text exactly in half by a vertical line:

MEMT   NGTX | ETEO   IHQZ

Now read the original message by checking off the first letter of the left half, the first letter of the right half, the second letter of the left half, the second letter of the right half, and so on. Ignore the three nulls at the ends. It is easy to guess where the spacings belong between words.

You can vary the rail fence cipher, if you like, by copying the two rows in reverse order, or by copying one row forward and the other backward. The decoding procedure, which you can easily work out for yourself, has to be changed accordingly.

Other variations can be obtained by writing the letters in a zigzag of more than two lines. For example, a 3-line rail fence cipher would begin like this:

```
M   M   N   T
 E T E O I H Q Z
 E   T   G   X
```

And encode:

MMNT ETEO IHQZ ETGX

The best way to understand a cipher is to use it for decoding an actual message. Throughout the book you will find "Practice Riddles" with coded answers that can be read only by deciphering them. *Please* do not try to do this directly on the book's pages. Copy the coded answer on a sheet of paper, then do all your work on that sheet. In this way you won't deface the book and spoil the fun for the next reader (if it is a library book), or for a friend who may wish to borrow your book.

What goes "Tee, he, he, he, he, plop!"?

AALU   HNHS   EDFY   MNAG   IGIH   AOFZ.

(This is a two-row, rail fence cipher. Read from left to right.)

2 · The Twisted Path Cipher

This is an elaboration of the letter-scrambling technique of the rail fence cipher. It uses a rectangular grid, or "matrix" as we will call it, which is simply a checkerboard of empty squares, or cells. Let's take a slightly longer sample message than the previous one:

MEET ME THURSDAY NIGHT

The message has 19 letters. As before, we add enough nulls (in this case only one is needed) to make a multiple of 4. For the 20 letters it will be convenient to use a 4-by-5 matrix. The message, with a null X at the end, is written in the 20 cells, from left to right, taking the rows from top to bottom:

M	E	E	T	M
E	T	H	U	R
S	D	A	Y	N
I	G	H	T	X

The next step is to trace on the matrix a particular path, the shape of which is agreed upon in advance by everyone who will be using the code. It is not a good idea to start the path by moving horizontally along the top row, left to right, because your cipher text would start with MEET, which would be recognized as a word and provide a clue to your system. A good path, called a "plow path" because farmers use this pattern to plow their fields, is shown below.

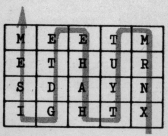

Copy the letters along the path, starting with the bottom cell on the right and following the curved line as it twists its way upward and leftward. The cipher text, written in groups of four, will be:

XNRM TUYT HAHE ETDG ISEM

To decipher, draw an empty 4-by-5 matrix, then fill in the cells with the letters of the cipher text. The first letter, X, goes in the lower right corner. N goes in the cell above it. Continue writing the letters along the same plow path that was used in coding the message. The message is read by taking each row from left to right, starting with the top row.

Another good path is a spiral. You can start the spiral at any corner cell and whirl inward, clockwise or counterclockwise, or you can begin at one of the central cells and spiral outward as shown below:

This spiral produces the cipher:

HUYA DTEE TMRN XTHG ISEM

If you want to make this code even harder to break, you can combine two different paths. For example: Write the message in the matrix along a plow path instead of left to right by rows. Then encode it by taking the letters along a spiral path. To decode, write the letters of the cipher text along the spiral path, then *read* them along the plow path.

Of course you and whoever receives the code must agree beforehand on the exact method to be used, as well as on the dimensions of the matrix. If you wish to vary the size and shape of the matrix with each message, you can put one number at the beginning of the cipher to indicate the height of the matrix, and another number at the end to indicate its width. This might, however, tip off the enemy that you are using a matrix to scramble the letters. You could use a secret ink (see Chapter 6) to put 4-5 in a corner of the sheet, or to put dots over the fourth and fifth letters of the message, or some other system of your own invention.

Paths do not have to be continuous. You can take the columns in order, from right to left, starting each column at the bottom, for example, and moving upward. Diagonals can also be used for paths, either broken or continuous. You can go up each diagonal from left to right:

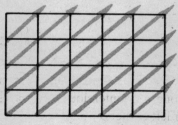

Or you can follow a diagonal plow path:

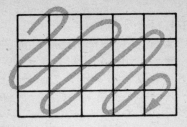

Indeed, you can adopt any type of path you like as long as everyone who sends and receives the cipher knows exactly what kind of path (or paths) is being used.

PRACTICE RIDDLE 2

What is gray, lives in a tree, and is terribly dangerous?

INEG   UNHT   RIUQ   SARH   AMAC   IWLE

(A 4-by-6 matrix was filled by writing left to right, from top to bottom. Then the answer was encoded along a counterclockwise spiral beginning at the lower left corner.)

3 · Scrambling with a Key Word

This is a subtle and historically important variation of the previous transposition method. Instead of using regular paths, broken or continuous, a "key word" is employed for mixing up the columns of a matrix in a completely haphazard way.

We will explain how it works by using the same message as before and the same 4-by-5 matrix. First the message is written in the 20 cells according to an agreed-upon plan. Let's assume it is along a clockwise spiral:

We now wish to scramble the order of the columns. To do this, we could simply number the columns from 1 to 5, but mix up the digits. Our key number would be, say 25143. Numbers, however, are not easy to remember, and that is where the key word comes in.

Any five-letter word, with no two letters alike, can serve as the key. Let's use the name FRANK. If we number these letters in the order in which they appear in the alphabet, A will be 1, F will be 2, K will be 3, N will be 4, and R will be 5.

$$\begin{matrix} 2 & 5 & 1 & 4 & 3 \\ F & R & A & N & K \end{matrix}$$

In this simple way, FRANK produces the five-digit number 25143. Write the five digits above the columns of the matrix:

2	5	1	4	3
M	E	E	T	M
Y	N	I	G	E
A	X	T	H	T
D	S	R	U	H

The digits tell us the order to follow in copying the columns from top down. Copy first the column headed 1, then the column headed 2, and so on to column 5. The cipher text will be:

EITR MYAD METH TGHU ENXS

The person who receives the cipher knows that the key word is FRANK, from which he quickly derives the number 25143. He draws the empty matrix, puts the digits above the columns, then copies the cipher vertically in each column, in the order indicated by the digits. After filling columns 1 and 2, his matrix will look like this:

2	5	1	4	3
M		E		
Y		I		
A		T		
D		R		

When all the cells are filled, the message is read along the agreed-upon clockwise spiral path. The advantage of this method is that it does not use simple and regular paths which could be guessed by a clever enemy who might "intercept" (as cryptographers like to say) the cipher text. Instead, it furnishes a haphazard broken path which is hard to discover unless one knows both the system and the key word.

Key words are so easy to remember that you and your friends can change the cipher every week by just picking a new word. A rectangular matrix of any size or shape can be used, but of course the key word must have the same number of letters as there are matrix columns. Using key words, or key phrases, to "randomize" cipher texts is an ancient but valuable technique. It is still used today in many of the elaborate cipher systems employed by nations throughout the world.

PRACTICE RIDDLE 3

What is gray and has four legs, a tail, and a trunk?

MTZG UIPI AANO ORXN SEGO

(This uses the matrix and the procedure just described, except the key word is JANET.)

CHAPTER 2

Easy
Substitution
Ciphers

In the ciphers discussed in the previous chapter, all the letters of a message remain the same when encoded. Only the order of the letters is changed. In a substitution cipher, the order of letters stays the same, but for each letter a different letter, or perhaps some kind of symbol, is used. Such ciphers are called substitution ciphers because something is substituted for every letter of the message. Substitution and transposition ciphers can be combined in all sorts of ways, but then the code becomes overly complicated and it is easy to make mistakes in encoding and decoding. (Professional cryptographers, by the way, restrict the word "code" to secret writing in which entire words or phrases are substituted for other words, listed in a special codebook. However,

14

in this book we will follow the common practice of using "code" as another word for cipher.)

Most of the following substitution ciphers are known as "monoalphabetic" (or single alphabet). This means that, for every letter, one and only one letter (or symbol) is substituted. If the code letter for T is K, then whenever there is a K in the cipher text it means T, and no other letter in the text can mean T.

There is a big advantage in having a method of substitution that is easy to remember. If you and your friends have to carry around a complete alphabet key, someone might find it and steal it. He could then read all your coded messages. This has actually happened many times in history. A spy will manage to steal an alphabet key or make a copy of it. The secret cipher becomes, of course, totally worthless. But if the cipher system is kept only in your head, no one can steal it.

One of the simplest and oldest substitution ciphers is created by writing the alphabet forward, then underneath, the alphabet is written backward:

A B C D E F G H I J K L M N O P Q R S T U V W X Y Z

Z Y X W V U T S R Q P O N M L K J I H G F E D C B A

Each letter stands for the letter directly below (or above) it. A message such as **MYRTLE HAS BIG FEET** would be written:

NBIGOV SZH YRT UVVG

15

or, if you group the letters in quadruplets:

NBIG   OVSZ   HYRT   UVVG

Note how the word "big" reappears near the beginning of the cipher text. It is just a coincidence, but amusing coincidences of this sort are very common in cipher writing. Sometimes they cause a lot of trouble for cryptanalysts because they are taken as clues. Of course they only lead the analysts off into false trails.

Another simple method is to number the letters of the alphabet forward (A = 1, B = 2, C = 3, and so on) or number them backward (A = 26, B = 25, C = 24, and so on). The numbers are used instead of letters. Dashes should go between the numbers to distinguish one-digit numbers from two-digit numbers.

Both these methods—the backward alphabet and the numbers in sequence—are too risky to use. They are so well known that your enemy is likely to know them, too. It takes only a minute or two to test a cipher to see if such a simple substitution method was employed. The systems that follow are much superior.

1 · Shift Ciphers

These are often called Caesar ciphers because the great Roman emperor Julius Caesar used them for secret government messages. They are easy to encode and decode.

A key number, known only to you and your friends (and which can be varied from time to time), tells you how far to shift a second alphabet when it is written underneath the first one. Suppose the key number is 7. Write the alphabet in a row. Put your pencil point on A and count seven letters to the right, starting on B and ending on H. Put A above H. Continue to the right with B, C, D, . . . until you reach Z, then go back to the beginning and finish the alphabet. Your 7-shift cipher will look like this:

```
T U V W X Y Z A B C D E F G H I J K L M N O P Q R S
A B C D E F G H I J K L M N O P Q R S T U V W X Y Z
```

To encode a message, find the letter in the top row and substitute for it the letter immediately below. Each letter in MYRTLE shifts forward seven letters to become TFYASL. To decode, find the letter in the bottom row and write the letter above it.

Needless to add, in this and other ciphers that use simple alphabet keys, you must always completely destroy the key after you have encoded or decoded a message. If you don't, someone might find the key, in a wastebasket perhaps, and learn the secret of your code.

Occasionally a word, by sheer coincidence, becomes another word when it is shifted. A good example is the word COLD. Try encoding it in a 3-shift cipher and you'll be surprised by what you get. What happens to PECAN in a 4-shift cipher? To SLEEP in a 9-shift? Try them and find out! It's fun to look for words that become other words in a shift cipher. Of course, the longer a word the less likely that a letter shift will produce another word. One of the longest of such words in English is ABJURER. In a 13-shift cipher it becomes NOWHERE.

PRACTICE RIDDLE 4

What did Mr. MacGregor buy a roll of Scotch Tape for?

SVSGL   PRAGF

What did he *want* it for?

GRA   PRAGF

(This is a 13-shift cipher.)

2 · Date Shift Ciphers

To make a shift cipher harder to break, you can vary the amount of the shift from letter to letter. There are many ways to do this. One clever way is to use the date on which you send the message as your key.

For example, assume you sent a message on October 21, 1973. October is the tenth month of the year. The date can be written: 10-21-73. Eliminate the dashes and you have the number 102173. Write this number repeatedly over the message:

```
102173   102   173   1021
MYRTLE   HAS   BIG   FEET
```

To encode the message, shift M forward one letter. It becomes N. (When the shift numbers are small, it is easy to learn how to make all the shifts in your head without having to write down two rows of the alphabet.) Y is to be shifted a zero distance, so it just stays Y. R moves ahead two letters to become T, and similarly with the other letters. Remember, if a shift carries you past Z, go back to A and continue the count.

The final cipher message, using 102173 as the key and spacing the letters in groups of four, will be:

```
NYTU   SHIA   UCPJ   GEGU
```

To decode, write the key number over the cipher text, the same way you did for encoding, then shift each letter *backward* in the alphabet by a distance indicated by the digit above it. Whenever a back

19

shift takes you beyond A, go to Z and continue the backward count.

Note that the cipher is not a monoalphabetic one. The last quadruplet, for example, stands for FEET. But the two E's in "feet" are represented by different letters, and the two G's in GEGU represent different letters. It is this which makes the date-shift cipher harder to crack. As we shall learn in Chapter 4, a cipher of this type is called polyalphabetic.

You don't have to use the date to provide the key number for a variable shift cipher. Any number will do, and you can remember the key number by using a key word as explained in Chapter 1, code 3.

PRACTICE RIDDLE 5

What did Paul Revere say when he finished his midnight ride?

AIWE !

(Use the date of Paul Revere's ride, April 18, without the year.)

3 · Key Word Ciphers

Here is a simple way to construct a substitution cipher alphabet by using a key word or phrase. Suppose you and your pals agree that the week's key word is JUPITER. Write the alphabet in a row. Underneath, write JUPITER, followed by all the *other* letters in alphabetical order:

```
A B C D E F G H I J K L M N O P Q R S T U V W X Y Z
J U P I T E R A B C D F G H K L M N O Q S V W X Y Z
```

Key words are easy to remember, and each word automatically produces a different substitution cipher. The procedures for encoding and decoding are the same as those of the previous ciphers in this chapter.

Note that V, W, X, Y, and Z are unchanged by this cipher alphabet. That is because JUPITER does not contain a letter which appears in the alphabet beyond U. If you use a key word that contains Y, it will change all the letters except Z. Of course your key word must not have duplicate letters.

If a key word is changed from week to week, sometimes it is not easy for everyone to get together to agree on the next key word. One way to avoid this is by using a book or a magazine to provide key words. If it is a book, everyone using the cipher must own or have easy access to a copy. If it is a magazine, pick a popular magazine, easily obtainable, and always use the issue currently on sale.

Select a good key word that appears somewhere in the book or magazine. Then write down the page number, the number of the line from the top of the page, and the number of the word in the line. These three numbers, separated by dashes, can be put at the end of your cipher text to let the receiver know how to find the key word in the book or magazine. If he sees 205-17-8 he turns to page 205, counts to the seventeenth line, and notes the eighth word in that line. The numbers will be meaningless to anyone who does not know what book or magazine is being used.

PRACTICE RIDDLE 6

What flower's name tells what the teacher did when she sat on a thumbtack?

MJNS

(The key word is THURSDAY.)

4 · The Pigpen Cipher

This cipher gets its name from the way in which letters are separated by lines, like pigs in a pen. It is also known as the Masons' cipher because the Society of Freemasons used it more than a hundred years ago. Confederate soldiers are said to have used it during the Civil War.

Draw two ticktacktoe patterns and two X patterns, alternating them as shown on the following page. A dot is placed in each compartment of the last two patterns.

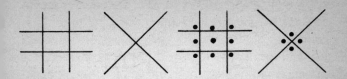

The alphabet is now printed inside the 26 compartments. Because this cipher is still very popular, especially with young people, it is a good idea to write the alphabet in some unusual order of letters which only you and your friends know.

C	F	I
B	E	H
A	D	G

(M K J pattern in X)

P.	S	.V
O	.R.	.U
N	Q.	T

(Y Z X W pattern in X)

In the above system, the alphabet goes upward in each column of the ticktacktoe patterns (taking the columns left to right), and counterclockwise in the X patterns, starting at the bottom compartment.

A message is encoded by substituting for each letter a tiny drawing of the compartment, with or without a dot, that contains the letter. This is how SEND ME TWO DOLLARS looks in the pigpen code:

ᴚᴏᴏꓵ⊓ >ᴏ ᖴ∆ᴐ ⊓ᴐᴠᴠꓶᴏᴚ

23

What's the end of everything?

FCO VOFFOO Γ

5 · The Polybius Checkerboard

Polybius was an ancient Greek writer who first proposed a method of substituting different two-digit numbers for each letter. The alphabet is written inside a 5-by-5 square matrix which has numbered rows and columns:

	1	2	3	4	5
1	A	B	C	D	E
2	F	G	H	I	J
3	K	L	M	N	O
4	P	Q	R	S	T
5	U	V	W	X	Y/Z

Note that both Y and Z are written in the last cell to divide the letters evenly. The context of the message should make clear which of the two letters is intended.

To encode, substitute for each letter the numbers marking the row and column in which the letter appears. Always put the row number first. For example, the number for J is 25. The word WATER-MELON would be encoded as:

53 - 11 - 45 - 15 - 43 - 33 - 15 - 32 - 35 - 34

To decode, simply locate each letter indicated by the number. The first number, 53, tells you to find the letter at the intersection of the fifth row and the third column.

PRACTICE RIDDLE 8

If you stand so that you face east and your back is to the west, what is on your left hand?

21 - 24 - 34 - 22 - 15 - 43 - 44

6 · Random Substitution Ciphers

All the substitution ciphers so far considered make use of cipher alphabets written according to a simple plan. The advantage is, as we have said before, that you don't have to carry the alphabet key around with you. It is easy to write or draw it each time you encode or decode.

A random substitution cipher is one that is constructed without a plan. You merely write the alphabet, and next to each letter you put any letter, number, or symbol you wish. Although you run the risk of losing the alphabet keys, random substitution ciphers are harder to crack than ciphers based on a simple system.

Dozens of detectives stories and novels have been written in which random ciphers play an important role in the plot. One of the best known is Arthur Conan Doyle's short story "The Adventure of the Dancing Men," in which Sherlock Holmes breaks a random cipher using stick figures of men for each letter of the alphabet. The most famous such story is Edgar Allan Poe's "The Gold Bug." The cipher in Poe's story uses numbers and various printer's symbols.

You can make up your own random cipher by writing the alphabet and pairing each letter with any sort of symbol you choose. The alphabet key shown below is typical. If you use it for encoding MERRY CHRISTMAS AND HAPPY NEW YEAR, the cipher text will look very mysterious:

The strange symbols do not, however, make the cipher any harder to crack than letters or numbers. The next chapter will give some elementary advice on how a cryptanalyst goes about solving such a code when he doesn't know the alphabet key that was used.

A = ↓   J = Ƶ   S = ←

B = ▽   K = ✶   T = π

C = φ   L = ↗   U = Ɲ

D = ⧣⧣⧣   M = ☉   V = #

E = ☉   N = ↙   W = ⊖

F = ⊬   O = □   X = ∾

G = △   P = ↑   Y = ⊨

H = →   Q = $ Z = ↑

I = Ⅱ   R = 卐

PRACTICE RIDDLE 9

What goes "Zzub, zzub, zzub"?

↓ ▽ ☉☉ ⊬ ↗ ⊨ Ⅱ ↙ △
▽ ↓ φ ✶ ⊖ ↓ 卐 ⧣⧣⧣ ←

27

7 · The Shadow's Code

In the 1930's a mysterious crime-fighter called the Shadow was the hero of a popular pulp magazine and an even more popular radio show. Dressed all in black, the Shadow could glide unseen through the darkness to battle the forces of evil. Stories about the Shadow, written by Maxwell Grant (pseudonym for the Shadow's creator, Walter B. Gibson), often contained curious codes. This

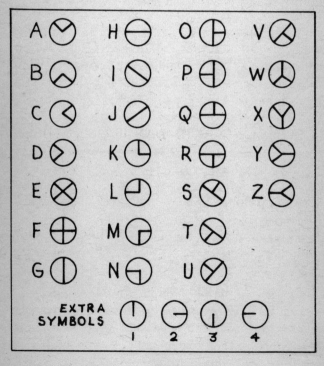

cipher, from a novelette called *The Chain of Death,* is one of the best.

In the alphabet key shown on the preceding page, note the four "extra symbols" at the bottom. These are inserted at *any* spot in the cipher text. Each symbol indicates how the sheet, on which the cipher text is written, is to be turned for encoding or decoding all the symbols that follow until the next extra symbol is reached.

Think of the line inside each extra symbol as a pointer that shows whether the top of the paper should be up, down, left or right. For example, if extra symbol 3 appears, the paper is turned upside down. Symbol 2 means that the page is turned so its top edge is on the right. Symbol 4 tells you to turn the sheet so its top edge is on the left. The first symbol means that the paper is in normal position, its top edge at the top.

The message: I AM IN DANGER. SEND HELP could look like this:

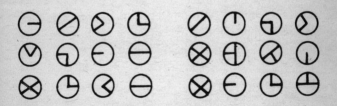

The first symbol tells you to give the page a quarter-turn clockwise before you decode the next four symbols. Then you come to another extra symbol which tells you to turn the page to normal position until you reach the next extra symbol. This constant turning of the sheet, while the alphabet key remains always in the same position, is a novel "twist" that makes this a most confusing cipher to any enemy who may intercept it.

PRACTICE RIDDLE 10

If two is company and three is a crowd, what are four, five, and six?

A message in the Dancing Men cipher,
solved by Sherlock Holmes

"Why, Holmes, it is a child's drawing," cried Dr. John Watson when he first saw the above figures penciled on a page torn from a notebook. But Sherlock Holmes recognized it immediately as a substitution cipher. The message is: AM HERE ABE SLANEY. The little flags mark the ends of words.

"I am fairly familiar with all forms of secret writing," Holmes declared, "and am myself the author of a trifling monograph upon the subject, in which I analyze one hundred and sixty separate ciphers. . . ."

```
5 3 ‡ ‡ † 3 0 5 ) ) 6 * ; 4 8 2 6 ) 4 ‡ .
) 4 ‡ ) ; 8 0 6 * ; 4 8 † 8 ¶ 6 0 ) ) 8 5
; I ‡ ( ; : ‡ * 8 † 8 3 ( 8 8 ) 5 * † ; 4 6
( ; 8 8 * 9 6 * ? ; 8 ) * ‡ ( ; 4 8 5 ) ; 5
* † 2 : * ‡ ( ; 4 9 5 6 * 2 ( 5 * – 4 ) 8 ¶
8 * ; 4 0 6 9 2 8 5 ) ; ) 6 † 8 ) 4 ‡ ‡ ; I
( ‡ 9 ; 4 8 0 8 I : 8 : 8 ‡ I ; 4 8 † 8 5
; 4 ) 4 8 5 † 5 2 8 8 0 6 * 8 I ( ‡ 9 ; 4 8
; ( 8 8 ; 4 ( ‡ ? 3 4 ; 4 8 ) 4 ‡ ; I 6 I
; : I 8 8 ; ‡ ? ;
```
The substitution cipher in Poe's tale "The Gold Bug"

It was supposedly written by the pirate Captain
Kidd, using invisible ink on parchment. Word divisions are not indicated. The message, which tells
where a treasure is buried, is:

> *"A good glass in the bishop's hostel
> in the devil's seat—forty-one degrees
> and thirteen minutes—northeast and by
> north—main branch seventh limb east
> side—shoot from the left eye of the
> death's-head—a bee-line from the tree
> through the shot fifty feet out."*

CHAPTER 3

How
to Break
Substitution
Ciphers

Solving simple substitution ciphers quickly is an
art that requires a great deal of knowledge and ex-
perience. In this chapter we will give a few pointers
and show how one goes about solving the type of
cryptogram that appears as a daily word puzzle in
many newspapers, and weekly in *The Saturday Review*. Such cryptograms have the original spacing
between words. Punctuation marks—periods, com-
mas, question marks and so on—are also shown
to make solving easier.

First, some important facts about the English
language:

1. The most often used letter is E, followed (in
order of frequency) by T, A, O, N. (E is also the

most common letter in German, French, Italian and Spanish, but in many other languages it is not. In Russian, for instance, O is the most used letter.)

2. The most common letter at the end of a word is E.

3. The most common beginning letter of a word is T.

4. A single-letter word is A or I, and on rare occasions, O.

5. The most frequent two-letter word is OF, followed by TO and IN.

6. The most used three-letter word is THE. The next most common is AND.

7 Q is always followed by U.

8. The consonant that most often follows a vowel is N.

9. The most common double letters are, in order of frequency, LL, EE, SS, OO, TT, FF, RR, NN, PP and CC.

10. The most frequently occurring four-letter word is THAT.

Note: THAT has the same letter at the beginning and at the end. When one or more letters appear more than once in a word, it is called a "pattern word." In solving a cryptogram, pattern words provide invaluable clues.

For example, suppose you saw the word XPP in a cryptogram. It is most likely to be a common word such as ALL, SEE or TOO, although it could be a less common word such as ODD, ADD, BOO,

INN, EGG, ZOO and scores of others. As we have learned, XYZX is most likely to be THAT.

A five-letter pattern such as BDCKC is probably THERE, or WHERE, or THESE, although it could be hundreds of less common words, such as NIECE, ROSES, NOSES, OMAHA, or IRENE.

The pattern ABCDB is probably WHICH. RDMMRJ is a pattern word in which two letters, R and M, are repeated. LITTLE is the best bet. Much less likely possibilities include SNEESH, SWOOSH, and TWEETS.

A skilled solver of cryptograms will quickly recognize pattern words such as TOMORROW, PEOPLE, BANANA, BEGINNING, COMMITTEE, and many, many others. If the cryptogram is a quotation, followed by the author's last name, an old hand at solving cryptograms would immediately recognize RBKJDRLDKMD as SHAKESPEARE.

One of the most valuable of all tools for an amateur cryptographer is a table of the most common pattern words, arranged so that you can find a pattern quickly and learn the words that are most likely to fit. A brief list of this sort is included in Fletcher Pratt's book (see bibliography). The most complete lists (for all the major languages of the world) are in the programs of the big electronic computers used by government cryptanalysts. In 1971 Jack Levine, a professor of mathematics at North Carolina State University, privately published a list of 184,000 pattern words from two through nine letters. The work was done by computer and was extended in 1972 by two more volumes covering words of ten through sixteen letters. Nonpattern words are not included, but in 1957 Levine published *A List of Words Containing No Repeated Letters*.

Another useful word list for cryptographers is a "reverse dictionary" in which words are spelled backwards and alphabetized. For instance, if you knew a word ended in CION you would look up all the words beginning with NOIC. A. F. Brown, a professor of linguistics at the University of Pennsylvania, directed the compilation of just such a dictionary. It was published in 1963, in eight bulky volumes, as the *Normal and Reverse English Word List*. There are more than 350,000 entries. The set is obtainable from the U.S. Department of Commerce, National Technical Information Service, 5285 Port Royal Road, Springfield, Virginia 22151, at ten dollars per volume.

It is hard to believe, but similar reverse dictionaries have also been published in recent decades in France, Greece, Russia, Italy, and perhaps other countries.

The technique of solving a cryptogram consists of making the best guesses you can about certain words, then substituting the letters throughout the cipher text to see if your guesses make sense or if they lead to an impossible combination of letters. If the latter happens, you have made an incorrect guess and will have to try something else. "The Gold Bug" contains an excellent description of how to crack a cryptogram, and you will find more detailed advice in *Cryptanalysis,* by Helen Gaines (see bibliography).

Let's analyze a simple, well-known quotation from the work of a famous English author:

ZU HO UD CUZ ZU HO ZSGZ AE ZSO JKOEZAUC

This cryptogram is so short that we cannot rely on the fact that the most common letter in it is E. A good starting point is the pattern word ZSGZ. As we have learned, the most common four-letter word is the pattern word THAT. Let's try it and see how it works out.

```
 T                T  T    THAT        TH         T
ZU  HO  UD  CUZ  ZU  HO  ZSGZ  AE  ZSO  JKOEZAUC
```

We are probably on the right track because ZSO now has to be THE and ZU is almost certainly TO. Adding the new letters, E and O, gives us:

```
TO   E  O   OT  TO   E  THAT        THE        E T O
ZU  HO  UD  CUZ  ZU  HO  ZSGZ  AE  ZSO  JKOEZAUC
```

The fourth word ends in OT. There are many possibilities. C, the first symbol of the word, cannot be H because H has already been used for another letter. Note that the last word of the cryptogram ends in C. TION is a very common ending for

words. If we substitute TION on the last word, C
becomes N and that would make CUZ translate as
the common word NOT. Adding the new letters, I
and N, continues to make good sense:

```
TO    E  O   NOT  TO   E  THAT  I   THE    E TION
ZU   HO  UD  CUZ  ZU  HO  ZSGZ  AE  ZSO   JKOEZAUC
```

AE cannot be IT, because T is already in our
translation. IF doesn't fit well between THAT and
THE, but IS does, so we add S to the solution:

```
TO    E  O   NOT  TO   E  THAT  IS  THE    ESTION
ZU   HO  UD  CUZ  ZU  HO  ZSGZ  AE  ZSO   JKOEZAUC
```

At this point you can probably complete the
final solution: TO BE OR NOT TO BE THAT IS
THE QUESTION. It is the famous line spoken by
Hamlet in Shakespeare's play of the same name. Of
course this was an easy cryptogram to solve. All our
guesses proved to be correct. There were no false
hunches that made it necessary to erase letters and
try different possibilities. But this example should
give you the general idea of how to go about solving substitution codes.

Cracking cryptograms is great fun, and the more
ciphers you solve, the better you will get. At this
point I could devote several pages to cryptograms
for you to work on, but some readers of this book
will be reading a library copy and, unfortunately, not
everyone is considerate of a book's next reader.

There would be a great temptation for someone to solve the cryptograms by writing directly on the page, rather than taking the trouble to copy them on a sheet of paper. The pages would get so marked up that the library would not want to keep the book on its shelves.

The best plan, if you want to practice cryptogram solving, is to ask a friend or relative to make up a random cipher and write a code message for you to break. The longer the message the better. Whoever writes the code message may think that a long message would be tougher for you to solve, but of course the opposite is true. A one-word message, such as COME, would be impossible to solve in cipher form because it could be *any* word of four different letters.

Claude E. Shannon, an American mathematician who founded a branch of modern mathematics called communication theory, wrote an important paper in 1949 ("Communication Theory of Secrecy Systems," *Bell System Technical Journal,* October, 1949) in which he showed that if a cryptogram has 30 or more letters it is almost certain to have only one solution. But if it has 20 or fewer letters it is usually possible to find more than one solution.

You will discover that, when you are working on a long cryptogram and trying out various hunches, you eventually reach a point at which you suddenly are absolutely sure that you are right and that it is only a matter of time until you complete the solution. This, in its small way, is not much different from the stronger emotion a scientist feels when he realizes there is enough evidence to make his new theory correct. The famous German philosopher and mathematician Gottfried Wilhelm Leibnitz once observed that solving a cryptogram is very much like solving a problem in science. If a scientist has only two or three unrelated facts about nature that need to be explained by a theory, he can usually think of dozens of equally good theories, just as a cryptographer can think of dozens of solutions for one short word. But if there are a large number of facts to be explained, it is like having a long cryptogram to solve. It is not so easy to invent one theory to explain hundreds of different facts which were previously mysterious. When such a theory is invented, and it fits all these facts, it is probably correct for a reason that is curiously similar to the reason why a solution to a long cryptogram is probably correct if it fits all the symbols.

One of the greatest of recent scientific discoveries involved an actual code used by nature—the genetic code. This code carries a plan for the development of an entire living creature along two intertwined DNA molecules in the nucleus of every living cell. The genetic code has an alphabet of only four symbols, each standing for a different chemical. The four chemicals are arranged along the DNA molecule in groups of three. These triplets are the "words" of an incredibly long "sentence" which tells every cell in a growing organism exactly what it is supposed to do.

In a metaphoric sense, the laws of science can be regarded as the "pattern words" of the universe. "Nature's great book," wrote Galileo, "is written in mathematical symbols." Scientists are the cryptographers engaged in the slow, progressive cracking of nature's many, perhaps infinitely many, secret ciphers.

I have given only a few elementary hints about solving simple substitution ciphers, and then only when the word divisions are shown in the cipher text. The art of breaking other kinds of ciphers is much too complicated to discuss in this introductory book. If you want to go deeper into the art of the cryptanalyst, I recommend the books by Gaines, Wolfe, and Sinkov (see bibliography) for further reading.

Edgar Allan Poe, in "The Gold Bug" and also in an essay on cryptography, said that any cipher which "human ingenuity" could construct could also be broken by human ingenuity. Poe may be right if we add a few qualifications. It must be a practical cipher; that is, a method which does not take too long to encode and decode accurately. In addition, the cryptanalyst must have a sufficient amount of cipher text to work on, and sufficient time to work on it. If Poe considered all these factors, his theory has not yet been proved right or wrong.

So far in history, Poe seems to have been right. At this very moment our cryptanalysts may be reading every secret message of the Soviet Union and

Below is an illustration drawn by Rudyard Kipling for "The First Letter," one of the tales in his famous book for children *Just So Stories*. The picture shows an ivory tusk on which carved pictures tell a story about a girl named Taffimai. Kipling says that the strange symbols on the sides and at the bottom are magic Runic letters, but actually they are the symbols of a substitution cipher. Can you read Kipling's code?

Hints: There are many spelling peculiarities in the original text: YOU is represented by U, W is either omitted or replaced by OU. F replaces V, and I is used instead of Y. In addition, A, G, O and T have two symbols each, and H has three.

The text on the left side begins: THIS IS THE STORY OF TAFFIMAI, ALL RITTEN OUT ON AN OLD TUSK.

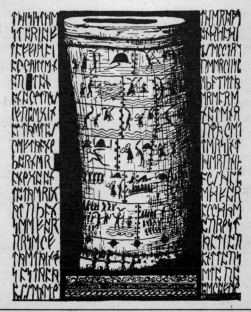

the Russians in turn may be reading every one of ours.

It is certainly possible, however, to create unbreakable ciphers that are impractical except in special instances. *The Codebreakers* devotes a chapter to a remarkable machine invented by an American named Gilbert S. Vernam. His device produces an uncrackable code because it uses what cryptographers call a "one-time system." This is a key that is completely random, and which is used only once and never again. In Kahn's excellent article on cryptology in *The Encyclopedia Americana,* he describes a simple "one-time system," pencil-and-paper cipher actually employed by Communist agents in World War II. It is truly unbreakable. Then why is it not often used? Because the great difficulty and expense of supplying new keys for every cipher message makes it impractical for general use.

CHAPTER 4

Hard-to-break Polyalphabetic Ciphers

The substitution ciphers of the previous chapters (except for the date-shift cipher) were all mono-alphabetic—one symbol for each letter. Such ciphers, as we have seen, are not difficult to solve, especially if the message is long, or if the crypt-analyst has many messages to work on. Because the Army, Navy, Air Force, State Department, and other branches of the government of any nation have to send many secret messages, they must use ciphers that are much more difficult to break than monoalphabetic substitution codes.

These difficult ciphers are called polyalphabetic (*poly* meaning *many*). This means that, throughout the cipher text, different symbols (letter or numbers) can stand for the same letter, and the same symbols can stand for different letters. Poly-alphabetic codes can be enormously complicated and extremely difficult to break. On the other hand, they must not be *too* complicated because then it takes too much time to encode and decode them accurately. The three following polyalphabetic ciphers are among the simplest and best.

1 · Porta's Digraphic Cipher

A digraphic cipher is one in which pairs of letters, instead of individual letters, provide the basis of the cipher text. In the Porta Cipher, a single symbol is substituted for every pair of letters in the message. The method was invented by Giovanni Battista Porta, an Italian writer, scientist and magician. At the age of 28 he published (in 1563) a delightful book on codes, which included this one. It is the first known digraphic cipher.

To use the cipher you need an enormous 26-by-26 square matrix. The alphabet is written outside the border, once across the top and once down the left side. The 676 cells are filled in any way you like—letters, numbers, or symbols—as long as no two cells are the same. In the example on pages 46–47, numbers from 1 through 676 are used. Porta himself used strange-looking symbols. If you are curious, a copy of his matrix is reproduced on page 139 of *The Codebreakers*.

Suppose you wish to encode the word THEY. The first pair of letters is TH. Find T in the vertical alphabet, then move along its row until you reach the column headed by H. The number at this intersection is 502, so that is the first symbol of the cipher text. In a similar manner, find 129 at the intersection of row E and column Y, the next pair of letters in the message. The first letter of every pair always gives the row, and the second letter gives the column. The cipher text for THEY is written 502-129.

To decode, for each number in the cipher text, substitute the pair of letters heading the row and column in which the number appears, always putting down first the letter heading the row.

To make the cipher harder to break, it would be best not to fill the matrix with 676 numbers in sequence. The numbers should be put in the cells in a random order, or 676 different symbols could be used, as Porta did. Another scheme would be to leave the numbers in sequence but scramble each of the alphabets. The first scheme makes the cipher harder to decode, and the second makes it harder to encode. Using both schemes together would make encoding and decoding such a chore that the cipher would be too inefficient for practical use.

PRACTICE RIDDLE 11

What Christmas greeting does A B C D E F G H I J K

M N O P Q R S T U V W X Y Z represent?

The answer is 353-116

	A	B	C	D	E	F	G	H	I	J	K	L	M
A	1	2	3	4	5	6	7	8	9	10	11	12	13
B	27	28	29	30	31	32	33	34	35	36	37	38	39
C	53	54	55	56	57	58	59	60	61	62	63	64	65
D	79	80	81	82	83	84	85	86	87	88	89	90	91
E	105	106	107	108	109	110	111	112	113	114	115	116	117
F	131	132	133	134	135	136	137	138	139	140	141	142	143
G	157	158	159	160	161	162	163	164	165	166	167	168	169
H	183	184	185	186	187	188	189	190	191	192	193	194	195
I	209	210	211	212	213	214	215	216	217	218	219	220	221
J	235	236	237	238	239	240	241	242	243	244	245	246	247
K	261	262	263	264	265	266	267	268	269	270	271	272	273
L	287	288	289	290	291	292	293	294	295	296	297	298	299
M	313	314	315	316	317	318	319	320	321	322	323	324	325
N	339	340	341	342	343	344	345	346	347	348	349	350	351
O	365	366	367	368	369	370	371	372	373	374	375	376	377
P	391	392	393	394	395	396	397	398	399	400	401	402	403
Q	417	418	419	420	421	422	423	424	425	426	427	428	429
R	443	444	445	446	447	448	449	450	451	452	453	454	455
S	469	470	471	472	473	474	475	476	477	478	479	480	481
T	495	496	497	498	499	500	501	502	503	504	505	506	507
U	521	522	523	524	525	526	527	528	529	530	531	532	533
V	547	548	549	550	551	552	553	554	555	556	557	558	559
W	573	574	575	576	577	578	579	580	581	582	583	584	585
X	599	600	601	602	603	604	605	606	607	608	609	610	611
Y	625	626	627	628	629	630	631	632	633	634	635	636	637
Z	651	652	653	654	655	656	657	658	659	660	661	662	663

	N	O	P	Q	R	S	T	U	V	W	X	Y	Z	
	14	15	16	17	18	19	20	21	22	23	24	25	26	A
	40	41	42	43	44	45	46	47	48	49	50	51	52	B
	66	67	68	69	70	71	72	73	74	75	76	77	78	C
	92	93	94	95	96	97	98	99	100	101	102	103	104	D
	118	119	120	121	122	123	124	125	126	127	128	129	130	E
	144	145	146	147	148	149	150	151	152	153	154	155	156	F
	170	171	172	173	174	175	176	177	178	179	180	181	182	G
	196	197	198	199	200	201	202	203	204	205	206	207	208	H
	222	223	224	225	226	227	228	229	230	231	232	233	234	I
	248	249	250	251	252	253	254	255	256	257	258	259	260	J
	274	275	276	277	278	279	280	281	282	283	284	285	286	K
	300	301	302	303	304	305	306	307	308	309	310	311	312	L
	326	327	328	329	330	331	332	333	334	335	336	337	338	M
	352	353	354	355	356	357	358	359	360	361	362	363	364	N
	378	379	380	381	382	383	384	385	386	387	388	389	390	O
	404	405	406	407	408	409	410	411	412	413	414	415	416	P
	430	431	432	433	434	435	436	437	438	439	440	441	442	Q
	456	457	458	459	460	461	462	463	464	465	466	467	468	R
	482	483	484	485	486	487	488	489	490	491	492	493	494	S
	508	509	510	511	512	513	514	515	516	517	518	519	520	T
	534	535	536	537	538	539	540	541	542	543	544	545	546	U
	560	561	562	563	564	565	566	567	568	569	570	571	572	V
	586	587	588	589	590	591	592	593	594	595	596	597	598	W
	612	613	614	615	616	617	618	619	620	621	622	623	624	X
	638	639	640	641	642	643	644	645	646	647	648	649	650	Y
	664	665	666	667	668	669	670	671	672	673	674	675	676	Z

PORTA'S CIPHER

2 · The Playfair Cipher

The Playfair cipher requires more work than Porta's cipher, to encode and decode, but it uses a much simpler matrix. It is named for Baron Lyon Playfair, a nineteenth-century Englishman, but actually was devised by the Baron's good friend Charles Wheatstone. A British scientist, Wheatstone became best known as a maker of musical instruments and for inventing a telegraphic system, even before it was independently invented by the American Samuel Morse. Telegraphic codes, such as the familiar Morse code, may be regarded as nonsecret ciphers in which patterns of dots and dashes are substituted for letters. Wheatstone devised his famous cipher for sending *secret* messages by standard telegraphic codes.

For many years the Playfair cipher was used by the British Army, especially during the Boer War. Australia used it in World War II. Dorothy L. Sayers' fictional detective Lord Peter Wimsey does a fine job of solving a Playfair cipher in the mystery novel *Have His Carcase*.

A Playfair matrix can be square or rectangular. We will use a 4-by-8 matrix, its 32 cells filled with the 26 letters and the digits from 2 through 7. (1 is left out because it is too easily confused with I.) The letters and the six digits are randomly placed in the cells. The pattern may look like this:

4	H	M	V	L	3	Y	D
X	K	B	5	P	Z	E	O
N	7	W	U	F	T	6	J
G	R	2	Q	C	A	I	S

As in Porta's cipher, the message is encoded by taking *pairs* of letters. There are three basic rules:

1. If both letters happen to be in the same *row*, use the letters immediately to the right of each letter. Think of the right end of each row as being joined to its left end. In other words, the letter to the "right" of the last letter in a row will be the first letter of that same row.

Example: PO is enciphered ZX.

2. If both letters are in the same *column*, use the letters immediately below each letter. Think of the bottom of each row as connected to its top. Thus the letter "below" a bottom letter is the top letter of that same column.

Example: CL is enciphered LP.

3. If the two letters are in different rows and in different columns, each letter is replaced by the letter in the *same row that is also in the column occupied by the other letter*.

That may sound confusing, but an example should make it clear. Suppose the letter pair is TH. Find T in the third row. H is in the second column. Put down 7 as the symbol for T because 7 is at the intersection of the third row and the second column.

Now we turn our attention to H. It is in the first row. T, its partner, is in the sixth column. At the intersection of the first row and sixth column is the digit 3, so this is the symbol we use for H. The cipher text for TH, therefore, is 73.

Let's try enciphering

I WILL ARRIVE AT FOUR P.M.

First, divide the message into letter pairs. If both letters of the same pair are alike, a null X is inserted between the letters. The division into pairs will be:

IW IL LA RX RI VE AT FO UR PM

Note that it was necessary to insert X between RR in ARRIVE, but not between LL in WILL. If only one letter remains at the end, another null X is added to make a final pair. In this case the final null was not required.

Using these three rules produces the following letter pairs, which make up the cipher. They are shown as "paired pairs" so that the cipher text will be in groups of four letters each.

26CY 3CGK 2SY5 3AJP 7QBL

It is deciphered in the same way that it is written

except for a slight modification when the two letters of a pair are in the same row or column. You must take letters immediately to the *left* of each letter, if both are in the same row, and letters immediately *above* if both are in the same column.

It is a marvelous cipher, easy to use, and hard to break. David Kahn, in *The Codebreakers*, tells an amusing story about it. When Playfair and Wheatstone tried to interest the British Foreign Office in the cipher, the Under Secretary complained that he could teach it in fifteen minutes to any elementary schoolboy of average intelligence.

"That's possible," said the Under Secretary, "but you could never teach it to attachés."

PRACTICE RIDDLE 12

Why did the hippopotamus stand on the marshmallow?

DJYK   JBFV   4J6T   C3YC   76ZJ   YKSP   SPGZ

3 · Lewis Carroll's Vigenère Cipher

This ingenious cipher is named for Blaise de Vigenère, a sixteenth-century Frenchman who invented many ciphers and wrote about them. Variations of the basic idea were later rediscovered by others. The version given here was invented by Lewis Carroll, the Oxford University mathematician who wrote *Alice's Adventures in Wonderland* and *Through the Looking-Glass*. Carroll published his cipher on a single card, anonymously, in 1868.

Carroll's 26-by-26 matrix is reproduced on page 53. This is the same size as Porta's matrix, but it is much easier to fill the cells because ordinary letters are used and they follow an easily remembered pattern. The first row is the standard alphabet from A to Z. Each succeeding row is the same alphabet except that it is shifted one letter to the left of the row preceding it.

The cipher requires a key word. In Carroll's brief instructions, he used the word VIGILANCE, illustrating the method with the message: MEET ME ON TUESDAY EVENING AT SEVEN.

The key word is written above the message, repeated as often as necessary:

```
V I G I L A N C E V I G I L A N C E V I G I L A N C E V I
M E E T M E O N T U E S D A Y E V E N I N G A T S E V E N
```

The letter above M, the first letter of the message, is V. Find the column of the matrix that is headed by V. Move down the column until you come to the row headed by M. The cipher letter at the intersection is H, so write down H as the first letter of the cipher text. The same procedure is followed with each letter of the message. The next letter is E. Above E is I. The intersection of the column headed by I, and the row headed by E, is

	A	B	C	D	E	F	G	H	I	J	K	L	M	N	O	P	Q	R	S	T	U	V	W	X	Y	Z	
A	a	b	c	d	e	f	g	h	i	j	k	l	m	n	o	p	q	r	s	t	u	v	w	x	y	z	**A**
B	b	c	d	e	f	g	h	i	j	k	l	m	n	o	p	q	r	s	t	u	v	w	x	y	z	a	**B**
C	c	d	e	f	g	h	i	j	k	l	m	n	o	p	q	r	s	t	u	v	w	x	y	z	a	b	**C**
D	d	e	f	g	h	i	j	k	l	m	n	o	p	q	r	s	t	u	v	w	x	y	z	a	b	c	**D**
E	e	f	g	h	i	j	k	l	m	n	o	p	q	r	s	t	u	v	w	x	y	z	a	b	c	d	**E**
F	f	g	h	i	j	k	l	m	n	o	p	q	r	s	t	u	v	w	x	y	z	a	b	c	d	e	**F**
G	g	h	i	j	k	l	m	n	o	p	q	r	s	t	u	v	w	x	y	z	a	b	c	d	e	f	**G**
H	h	i	j	k	l	m	n	o	p	q	r	s	t	u	v	w	x	y	z	a	b	c	d	e	f	g	**H**
I	i	j	k	l	m	n	o	p	q	r	s	t	u	v	w	x	y	z	a	b	c	d	e	f	g	h	**I**
J	j	k	l	m	n	o	p	q	r	s	t	u	v	w	x	y	z	a	b	c	d	e	f	g	h	i	**J**
K	k	l	m	n	o	p	q	r	s	t	u	v	w	x	y	z	a	b	c	d	e	f	g	h	i	j	**K**
L	l	m	n	o	p	q	r	s	t	u	v	w	x	y	z	a	b	c	d	e	f	g	h	i	j	k	**L**
M	m	n	o	p	q	r	s	t	u	v	w	x	y	z	a	b	c	d	e	f	g	h	i	j	k	l	**M**
N	n	o	p	q	r	s	t	u	v	w	x	y	z	a	b	c	d	e	f	g	h	i	j	k	l	m	**N**
O	o	p	q	r	s	t	u	v	w	x	y	z	a	b	c	d	e	f	g	h	i	j	k	l	m	n	**O**
P	p	q	r	s	t	u	v	w	x	y	z	a	b	c	d	e	f	g	h	i	j	k	l	m	n	o	**P**
Q	q	r	s	t	u	v	w	x	y	z	a	b	c	d	e	f	g	h	i	j	k	l	m	n	o	p	**Q**
R	r	s	t	u	v	w	x	y	z	a	b	c	d	e	f	g	h	i	j	k	l	m	n	o	p	q	**R**
S	s	t	u	v	w	x	y	z	a	b	c	d	e	f	g	h	i	j	k	l	m	n	o	p	q	r	**S**
T	t	u	v	w	x	y	z	a	b	c	d	e	f	g	h	i	j	k	l	m	n	o	p	q	r	s	**T**
U	u	v	w	x	y	z	a	b	c	d	e	f	g	h	i	j	k	l	m	n	o	p	q	r	s	t	**U**
V	v	w	x	y	z	a	b	c	d	e	f	g	h	i	j	k	l	m	n	o	p	q	r	s	t	u	**V**
W	w	x	y	z	a	b	c	d	e	f	g	h	i	j	k	l	m	n	o	p	q	r	s	t	u	v	**W**
X	x	y	z	a	b	c	d	e	f	g	h	i	j	k	l	m	n	o	p	q	r	s	t	u	v	w	**X**
Y	y	z	a	b	c	d	e	f	g	h	i	j	k	l	m	n	o	p	q	r	s	t	u	v	w	x	**Y**
Z	z	a	b	c	d	e	f	g	h	i	j	k	l	m	n	o	p	q	r	s	t	u	v	w	x	y	**Z**

LEWIS CARROLL'S CIPHER

M, so M is the second letter of the cipher text. The complete text is:

HMKB XEBP XPMY LLYR XIIQ TOLT FGZZ V

We could, of course, have added three nulls to the original message to make the cipher text end with a quadruplet of letters.

To decipher, a slightly different procedure is followed. As before, start by writing the key word repeatedly over the cipher text. The letter above H is V. Find the column headed by V. Move down the column until you reach H in the column, then move left along the row until you reach M, the first letter in the row as well as the label for that row. M is the first letter of the original message. The same procedure is followed for every letter.

It is impossible, Carroll wrote, "for anyone, ignorant of the key word, to decipher the message, even with the help of the table."

Well, not really. The code can be broken by experts, but it is not easy. In variant forms it continues to be one of the most popular codes ever devised.

There is another way to use the same matrix and key word. You may prefer it to Carroll's method because its procedure for decoding is exactly the same as the procedure for encoding. It is called the Beaufort system, named for Admiral Sir Francis Beaufort, of the British Royal Navy, who invented it. In 1857 it was sold for a sixpence in England as a system for sending secret messages by telegraph or by postcards.

We can see how it works by considering only M, the first letter of Carroll's message, and V, the key letter above it. Find M on the vertical alphabet outside the left border of the matrix. Move along row M until you come to V, then move up the column containing this V until you reach J, the letter at the top. J is used as the first letter of the cipher text.

Now see what happens when you decode this letter. Find J on the left, move along the row to V, as before, then up the column to the letter at the top. It is M!

PRACTICE RIDDLE 13
What did the baby porcupine say to the cactus?

XQZA   FPUT   LWEV?

(Use the Beaufort system with the key word FISH.)

CHAPTER 5

Simple
Code
Machines

Every technologically advanced country today uses computers for encoding and decoding. Above all, it uses computers for cracking enemy codes. Not only are they used for military and diplomatic intelligence, but large privately owned corporations now use computers for their own top-secret communications between officials of the same firm. Information from an American or Russian spy satellite is sent in a cipher which is translated almost instantly by sophisticated computer machines in the country that launched the satellite.

In World War II Japan had two codes. One was a worthless cipher written by hand, but the other was a very advanced code which used an ingenious typewriter (U.S. cryptanalysts called it the PURPLE machine) for encoding and decoding. Shortly before the attack on Pearl Harbor, our cryptanalysts succeeded in cracking the code. *The Chicago Tribune,* bitterly opposed to President Franklin D. Roosevelt, published the top-secret fact that we had broken this code. The Japanese leaders refused to believe it! For the rest of the war they continued to use their typewriter code. Of course we read all their messages and thereby secured enormous military advantages. You can read the details of this fascinating story in the first chapter of *The Codebreakers.*

We, too, had typewriter code machines in World War II. During the war I was a yeoman on the USS *Pope,* a destroyer escort which prowled the North Atlantic in search of German submarines. When the ship was decommissioned in Florida, to be put in "mothballs," the first piece of equipment taken from the ship was the code machine in our "radio shack." By now I would guess that the device is as obsolete as a model-T Ford.

There are, however, many extremely simple code devices which you can make, and also ways of using common machines for sending secret messages. The methods described in this chapter are the best I know.

1 · Typewriter Codes

An ordinary typewriter can furnish the basis for many simple substitution ciphers. For instance, instead of hitting the proper key for each letter, hit the key immediately above it and to the left. Or if you prefer, use the key immediately to the right, or the key above and to the right.

If you choose up and left, I LOVE YOU is typed like this:

8　09F3　697

And if you choose right:

O　:PBR　UPI

To make the code harder to crack, you can adopt such stratagems as alternating the two methods just explained, starting with above and left:

8　:9B3　U9I

The decoding technique, as usual, reverses the encoding procedure. If the code uses keys to the right on the typewriter keyboard, translate the cipher text by hitting keys to the *left* of each symbol, and similarly for the other methods.

PRACTICE RIDDLE 14

What do ghosts chew?

NPPN:R　HI,

(The cipher is typed with a right system.)

2 · A Telephone Dial Code

This clever code uses an ordinary telephone dial to provide an alphabet key. As you can see, the

A TELEPHONE DIAL

letters on the dial are in groups of three, with one number for each triplet.

To write in telephone code, find each letter on the dial. Then write down the number beside it. If the letter is the nearest to the front of the alphabet, among the three letters in the triplet, indicate this by drawing above the number a small line leaning to the left. If the letter is nearest to the end of the alphabet, slant the line to the right. If the letter is in the middle of the triplet, draw a vertical line.

Notice that Q and Z are the only letters not represented on the dial. Since the digits 1 and 0 have no letters beside them, you can use 1 to stand for Q and 0 to stand for Z.

I LOVE YOU looks like this in telephone dial code:

$$4\overset{\prime\prime}{5}\,\overset{\prime}{6}\,\overset{\prime}{8}\qquad \overset{\shortmid}{3}\,\overset{\prime}{9}\,\overset{\prime}{6}\,\overset{\prime\prime}{8}$$

PRACTICE RIDDLE 15

What's green and goes "chug, chug, chug"?

$$\overset{\backslash}{2}\,\overset{\prime}{6}\quad \overset{\prime}{6}\,\overset{\prime\backslash}{8}\,\overset{\backslash}{8}\,\overset{\prime}{2}\,\overset{\prime}{6}\,\overset{\backslash}{2}\,\overset{\prime}{7}\,\overset{\backslash}{3}\qquad \overset{\backslash}{7}\,\overset{\prime}{4}\,\overset{\prime}{2}\,\overset{\prime\prime}{5}\,\overset{\prime\prime}{5}\,\overset{\prime}{3}$$

3 · The Scytale

"Scytale" was the Latin name of the earliest known code device. It was first used by Spartans in the fifth century before Christ.

The scytale is nothing more than a cylinder made of wood or some other material. You and your friends must each have one of exactly the same size. It is possible to use ordinary pencils for scytales, but they are too thin to be convenient. Besides, the "enemy" has pencils too! It is best to obtain rods that are an inch or more thick. Cardboard tubes inside paper towels or bathroom tissue work very well.

To encode a message, take a long strip of paper and wrap it in spiral fashion around the cylinder. You can buy a roll of adding machine paper tape in any stationery store. It is ideal for the scytale. After the strip is wound, print the message in rows

that run the length of the cylinder, as shown in the
illustration. When the strip is unwrapped, the letters
are scrambled in the manner of a transposition
cipher.

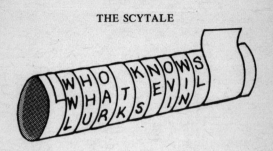

Decoding is easy. Just wrap the strip in the same
way around a scytale of the same size as the one
used in encoding. As David Kahn said in *The
Codebreakers,* the "words leap from loop to loop."

4 · The Alberti Disk

This simple wheel device, shown in the picture,
quickly provides 26 different substitution cipher
alphabets which you can use for hundreds of different kinds of substitution codes. The device is
easily made by cutting a disk out of cardboard and
mounting it on a sheet of cardboard with a paper
fastener through the center of the disk.

Note that the 26 inner letters are in alphabetical
order around the rim of the disk, but on the outside circle, on the cardboard backing, the letters

are randomly arranged. You and your friends must, of course, have wheels that are exactly alike.

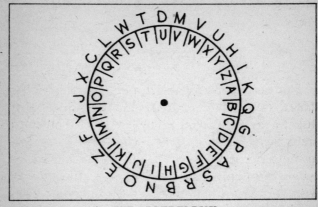

THE ALBERTI DISK

Before you send a message in code, turn the wheel until any letter you like is opposite the A on the rim of the disk. This outside letter is the first letter of your cipher text. From now on, the wheel remains in the same position. For each letter in the message, find the letter on the inside alphabet and use the letter that appears opposite it on the outside circle. The receiver of the message has only to set his wheel as you did, according to the key letter at the beginning of the cipher text. Then he can use the wheel to translate the cipher.

In the illustration, the wheel is set with K opposite A. Since there are 26 different letters to put opposite A, there are 26 different cipher alphabets to choose from. You can change the code each time you send a message. If the wheel is set as shown, the message, WHERE IS BOB, with a null X at the end, appears this way in groups of four letters:

KVBA   LANW   QJQU

This is a monoalphabetic cipher, which means that it is not hard to break. To use the Alberti disk for a polyalphabetic cipher, much harder to crack, simply turn the wheel after each letter, following any kind of system you like. One simple procedure is to move the wheel just one letter clockwise (or counterclockwise) after you encode each letter. You can easily think of more complicated procedures. For example, first turn the wheel one letter, next time turn it two letters, then three letters, then go back to one again. Keep repeating this 1-2-3-1-2-3-1-2-3 . . . series.

An even more complicated system is to turn the wheel according to a series of random digits, which are remembered by a key word, as explained in Code 3 of the first chapter. You will recall that we learned how the word FRANK stands for digits 25143. If everyone knows this key word, ciphers can be encoded by first rotating the wheel two letters, then five, then one, and so on, repeating the series given by the key number. With a little thought you can invent all sorts of ways of varying the procedure to make polyalphabetic codes that are almost impossible to crack. They should not be too complicated because then it will be hard to encode and decode quickly without a lot of errors.

The device was first invented by Leon Battista Alberti, a fifteenth-century Italian architect. His writings on codes have earned him the title "Father of Western Cryptology." Alberti's disk was reinvented many times in later centuries. Perhaps you once received an Alberti disk as a premium in a box of breakfast cereal. If so, you owned one of the oldest and most versatile mechanisms in the history of cryptography.

PRACTICE RIDDLE 16

What word does everybody in California pronounce wrong?

X Z R P G M

(Use the wheel shown in the picture, but with *A* set at *X*, as indicated by the first letter of the cipher text.)

5 · Thomas Jefferson's Wheel Cipher

A wonderfully ingenious method of constructing a polyalphabetic cipher, with the aid of many rotating disks, was invented by none other than Thomas Jefferson, the third president of the United States. Jefferson's "wheel cypher," as he called it, used 36 wooden wheels of the same size, mounted

on an iron rod, each wheel with a scrambled alphabet around its edge. The first illustration, reproduced
from David Kahn's book, shows a 25-wheel version
once used by the U.S. Army.

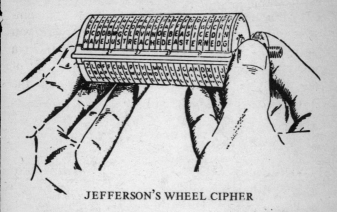

JEFFERSON'S WHEEL CIPHER

In the picture, the wheels have been set so that
the horizontal line of letters, above the cross-bar,
reads: "Have just reached eastern edg." These are
the first 25 letters of a message. The encoder copies
down *any* other horizontal line of letters. The decoder sets the wheels to align the cipher text, then
he looks around the cylinder for a line which makes
sense. All the other lines, Jefferson wrote, "will be
jumbled and have no meaning, so that he cannot
mistake the true one intended."

It is easy to make a simpler form of this device
by cutting out six disks of cardboard, of six different sizes, and mounting them on a sheet of cardboard as shown in the second picture. A long paper

fastener, through the centers of the disks, attaches them to the cardboard backing and allows all of them to rotate. The rim of each wheel has 26 compartments which contain the letters of the alphabet in a random order.

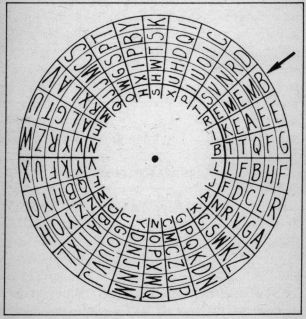

FLAT VERSION OF JEFFERSON'S WHEEL CIPHER

To send a cipher, first divide the message into groups of six letters each. Turn the disk until the first six letters are on a straight line, reading outward from the smallest disk toward the largest one. In the illustration, the arrow points to a line

66

that spells REMEMB. These are the first six letters of:

REMEMBER TO SEND MAP

Look around the wheels and you will see that no other straight "spoke" of six letters could be the beginning of an English sentence. There is a small chance, of course, that another line *might* make sense, but the probability of this happening is extremely low. The more disks you use, the lower the probability of such a coincidence and the easier it will be to recognize the correct line. Six wheels work fairly well. Ten are even better because then you can divide the text into groups of ten letters.

The next step is to copy down *any* of the other 25 "spokes" you please. For example, you could write the fourth line clockwise from REMEMB. It is:

JF D C L R

Now reset the wheels to spell, at any spoke of the wheels, the next six letters of the message: ER TO SE. Repeat the same procedure. For each group of six letters that you align on the wheels, choose any scrambled spoke you like and copy its six letters for your cipher text. Follow this procedure until the entire message is encoded.

To decode, the receiver divides the letters of the secret message into groups of six, then sets his disks so that the first six letters of the text, JFDCLR, are in line. He glances around the dials until he sees a line that makes sense. This procedure is repeated with each group of six letters until the entire message is decoded.

- Jefferson's wheel cipher is almost (not quite!) unbreakable. Kahn discloses that in 1922 it was reinvented and adopted by the U.S. Army. It is still used today, he adds, by the U.S. Navy.

PRACTICE RIDDLE 17

What would your nose be if it grew 12 inches long?

W   BJWR

(Use the wheels shown in the picture.)

6 · Grilles

A grille (sometimes called a grid) is a square or rectangular piece of cardboard or other material into which openings have been cut at various places. The basic idea of using such a grille for transposing letters or words goes back to Girolomo Cardano, a sixteenth-century Italian mathematician. Cardano used the grille in only one position. The letters (or words) of a message were written through the "windows," the grille was removed, and the spaces

5	6	7	8	9	5
9	2	3	4	2	6
8	4	1	1	3	7
7	3	1	1	4	8
6	2	4	3	2	9
5	9	8	7	6	5

HOW CELLS ARE NUMBERED FOR
MAKING A GRILLE

between those letters filled with null letters to make
a false message. When a similar grille was placed
over the coded message, the null letters were hidden
and the true letters could be read easily through the
holes.

Later, grilles were invented which could be rotated so that every cell of a matrix contained a letter
of the original message, but in a mixed-up order.
Such rotating grilles actually were used by the Germans for a short period near the end of World
War I.

To make a 6-by-6 grille, rule a square of cardboard into the 36-cell checkerboard shown in the
first picture. Number the cells as indicated. Cut out
any one cell with the number 1, another cell with
2, any other cell with 3, and so on, until the square
has nine cells missing. The grille may look like the
one shown in the second picture. We will call each
missing cell a hole or window even though two or

more open cells may be next to each other, forming a single opening.

Draw a square of the same size on a sheet of blank paper. Place the grille on this square in any position and print the first nine letters of the message in the nine holes. You can follow any procedure you like. For example, you can print the letters from bottom to top, taking the columns from right to left. Of course your friends must know the procedure, as well as the grille's first position.

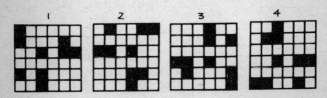

A GRILLE IN ITS FOUR POSITIONS

Now give the grille a quarter-turn clockwise, or counterclockwise if you prefer, and print the next nine letters, following the same procedure you did for the first nine letters. Another quarter-turn in the same direction permits you to add nine more letters, and a final turn allows nine more. If the message is shorter than 36 letters, it doesn't matter. You can stop lettering whenever you please. If longer than 36 letters, move the grille to another spot on the sheet, or use another sheet, and repeat the same operations until the entire message is encoded. The picture shows a grille rotated clockwise to provide four positions. If you study the picture, you will see that each position puts the nine holes over a different set of nine cells.

You could send the matrix itself, with its scrambled letters, but this is dangerous because, if it were intercepted, the enemy might guess from its appearance that you were using a grille. It is best to copy the letters on another sheet of paper, writing them in a row of quadruplets, so that there will be no clue about what kind of cipher system you used. Again, you can follow any copying procedure you wish, just so that all who use the code know the procedure.

Let's assume that you take the rows from top to bottom, copying each row from left to right, the way one reads ordinary printing. The person who receives the coded message first draws a 6-by-6 checkerboard of the proper size, then he writes the cipher text in the cells, taking each row left to right, and the rows from top to bottom. He places his duplicate grille over the checkerboard in the first position. The next step is to copy the letters in a row, this time taking the letters in each column from bottom to top, starting with the right-hand column and moving leftward for each new column (or following whatever procedure was agreed upon for putting the letters into the grille's windows). After the nine letters have been copied, he gives the grille a quarter-turn clockwise, to the second position, and copies the new set of nine letters. After two more turns of the grille, he will have written the

36 letters of the original message in their proper order.

It is, of course, a complicated transposition cipher. The grille is a mechanical device which automatically scrambles the letters for the encoder and just as efficiently unscrambles them for the decoder. Here is a secret message scrambled according to the procedures suggested above and using the grille shown in the illustration on page 69.

GSJT LHUK ESWL TILT EHSO HATE ATOS SEEO HAEH

Note, two words, "tilt" and "hate," have turned up by chance in the cipher text. They have nothing to do with the message!

If you have made a grille like the one shown in the picture, see how quickly you can use it for translating the cipher text.

Square grilles with any square number of cells can be made, but if the number of cells on a side is an odd number, as on a 5-by-5 or 7-by-7 grille, the center cell cannot be used. The reason is that, if a hole were cut in the center, the hole would stay at the same spot while the grille rotated. In such cases it is best not to cut a central hole. A null letter can be put in the center cell or, if your prefer, just leave that cell blank. It is a good idea to mark in some way the surface of a grille that is intended to be face up. It works just as well, of course, with either surface against the paper, which means that by turning over a grille you obtain a different grille.

It will be a mirror image of the former grille, and it produces a different cipher text. Therefore every grille actually can be used for two different cipher systems.

As an exercise in mathematics, see if you can figure out how to number the 64 cells of an 8-by-8 checkerboard so that you can make a grille with 16 windows which will catch all 64 cells when the grille is rotated.

The most famous novel in which a rotating square grille is used for a cipher is *Mathias Sandorff* (1885) by Jules Verne. The cipher text was left in matrix form. No cryptanalysis was needed because Verne's heroes realized they were confronted with a rotating square grille code and were able to find one of the grilles. Verne tells his readers that such a cipher is unbreakable unless you have the grille, a statement which shows how little Verne understood the art of cryptanalysis.

The next picture shows a grille of a different type. It is rectangular, with rectangular openings which allow you to print words instead of letters. Like the square grille, it also has four positions, but in two of the positions the grille must be *turned over* so that its other side is uppermost. A cut-off corner makes it easy to place the grille properly. As the picture shows, the first position has the cut-off corner in the upper left corner of the rectangle. When the grille is turned over from left to right, this corner moves to upper right. Now flip the grille from top to bottom so that the corner is at the lower

right; finally flip it right to left so that the corner is
at the lower left.

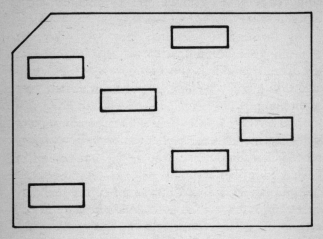

A TURN-OVER WORD GRILLE

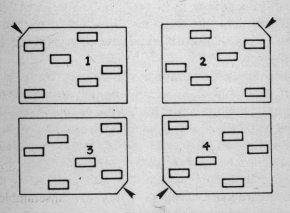

THE WORD GRILLE IN ITS FOUR POSITIONS

If you prefer, you can change these positions so that the cut-off corner circles the rectangle in a counterclockwise direction, or you can adopt some other ordering for the four positions.

The word grille pictured here will show six words in each position, or 24 words in all. As with the letter grille, it doesn't matter if the message is shorter because blank spaces won't affect the scrambling. If the message is longer than 24 words, the grille can be moved to another spot or another sheet of paper. There's nothing to prevent you from sending a very long message using many sheets of paper.

Each time you use the grille, either for encoding or decoding, it is a good practice first to run a pencil around its border to outline the shape of the grille. In this way you can be sure you are placing the grille properly in each of its four positions. If a word is too long to fit in a window, write part of it in one opening and the other part in the next opening. Two short words can be pushed together as a single word.

For the secret message shown on page 76, words were written in the windows from left to right and top to bottom, then the words were copied from the filled rectangle by taking them in the same left-right, top-bottom order, just as you do when you read a page in a book. Try making a turn-over grille by copying the large picture of the grille and cutting it out of cardboard. Then see if you can unscramble the 24 "words" in the following secret message:

```
FOR   ASCRAM   SEE  OFTHE   HOW  FASTEST   SENDING
BLED   METHODS   QUICKLY   MESS   SECRET   AGE   CODE
EVER   YOU  MESS   THIS   CAN   INVEN   DECODE   TED
AGES   ISONE.
```

Remember: You do not put the grille over the actual message. First you must draw a rectangle the same size as your grille. Place the grille on the rectangle, and by turning it to its four positions you can outline in pencil the 24 rectangular spots where the words go. Write the words of the scrambled message, from left to right, inside these spots. Now you can apply the grille and read the words in their proper sequence.

7 · The Triangle Code

To make this handy little coding device, first draw an equilateral triangle in the center of a sheet of paper. The alphabet, plus a circled period, is lettered in proper sequence around the outside of the triangle. The letters must be equally spaced as shown on the opposite page.

Draw an identical triangle on a sheet of thin cardboard. The alphabet, plus a circled period, is written on the edge of its three sides, but in a random order. Draw an arrow pointing to one of its corners. Cut out the cardboard triangle and place it on the paper triangle. The arrow should be pointing straight up, as shown in Fig. 1 opposite.

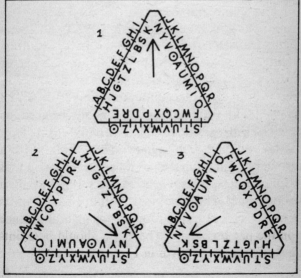

THE ROTATING TRIANGLE IN THREE POSITIONS

The outside alphabet (on the sheet of paper) is used for the letters of the message. The letters on the cardboard triangle are used for the cipher text.

Suppose you wish to encode SEND. With the arrow pointing up (position 1 in the second picture), find S in the outside alphabet. The letter on the cardboard triangle, opposite S, is F. Put this down as the first letter of the cipher text.

Turn the cardboard triangle clockwise and fit it on the other triangle so that its arrow points down and right. The second letter of SEND is E, which gives X as the cipher letter.

Another clockwise rotation produces the third position, with the arrow pointing down and left. N encodes as X again, which shows that the device is producing a polyalphabetic cipher. The next turn brings the triangle back to the first position. D encodes as T. The cipher text for SEND, therefore, is:

F X X T

To decode, follow the same procedure, always starting with position 1 and turning the triangle clockwise after each letter is decoded. Now, of course, you must find the cipher text letter on the cardboard triangle and copy the letter opposite it in the outside alphabet.

Similar cardboard devices shaped like squares, pentagons, or hexagons can be used for writing more complicated polyalphabetic ciphers. All these devices are really special modifications of Porta's cipher. Think about it and you will realize that Porta's disk, with one extra symbol to make 27 divisions of the circle (a multiple of 3), could be used for encoding and decoding the triangle cipher. You would rotate the wheel nine (27/3 = 9) letters after each letter is encoded or decoded. The cardboard triangle, however, enables you to do the same thing much easier and faster, and with less likelihood of making a mistake.

PRACTICE RIDDLE 18

What goes "99-thump, 99-thump, 99-thump"?

HCAA YOMX ӨZAO WRNX LPTX XVXM

CHAPTER 6

Invisible Writing

An ancient method of secret writing, entirely different from ciphers, is writing with inks that are invisible until something is done to "develop" the writing. The use of such inks is as old as civilization. Spies are still using them today.

The best secret inks are made with special chemicals not easily obtained except through chemical supply houses. Ink made with copper sulfate, for instance, turns red when exposed to ammonia fumes. Writing done with a colorless solution of iron sulfate becomes bright blue when it is cotton-swabbed with a solution of potassium cyanate, or brown when painted with a solution of washing soda (sodium carbonate). There are hundreds of other formulas for "sympathetic inks," as they are often called. The writing is developed by using another chemical called the "reagent." Some of these chemicals can be dangerous to use unless you are a chemist and take the proper precautions. The following methods of invisible writing are all safe and effective, and use substances that are easily obtained.

Professional spies seldom use invisible inks on sheets of blank paper because it would arouse suspicion if intercepted. Usually a false message is typed or written in the usual way, then the secret message is added between the lines in invisible ink. The message can also be written on the back of an innocent-looking letter or photograph, or in lines that cut across visible writing at an angle.

Another common trick is to swab separate letters, in a book or magazine, with invisible ink. When the book or magazine is received, the ink is developed and, by reading the marked letters in sequence, the original message is obtained.

Invisible writing can also be combined with a cipher. If the enemy suspects an invisible message and succeeds in developing it, he still will be unable to read it unless he knows or is able to crack the code.

1 · Inks That Develop When Heated

Almost any citrus fruit juice can be used as an invisible ink. It is better to write with a tiny paint brush than with a pen because pressure from the pen's point will make marks on the paper that often can be seen in slanted light. If you do use a pen, be sure the point is completely clean. Otherwise, some old ink on the point will mix with the sympathetic ink and make it visible. Also, be sure to use soft, uncoated paper so that the ink will soak into the fibers. If you use coated paper, such as high-quality bond typewriter paper, the liquid dries on the surface, and, like pressure marks, it can be seen in slanted light.

Inks made of citrus fruit juice are developed by heating the paper slowly over a hot light bulb. *Never* use actual fire. It is much too hot. The result is almost sure to be charred paper, or the paper may catch on fire. A 150-watt light bulb works best, but be careful not to hold the paper too close to the bulb or it will char, and you also might burn your fingers. Another method is to iron the sheet with a hot iron.

Lemon, orange, or grapefruit juice is as good as any substance you can use. Onion juice also works well. Like most invisible inks made with organic substances, the writing turns brown when it is heated gently.

2 · An Ink That Turns Red

Phenolphthalein is a white powder that, in a solution, turns deep red when mixed with an alkaline. Magicians use it for performing "water to wine" tricks.

A drugstore probably won't sell you pure phenolphthalein, but it is the chief ingredient of many laxatives which you *can* buy. Ex-Lax, for instance. It makes an excellent sympathetic ink. Mash one tablet up thoroughly in about half an ounce of rubbing alcohol. Be sure the entire tablet is dissolved.

Use a brush to print the secret message. The writing will be invisible when the ink dries. To develop it, moisten a piece of cotton or cleansing tissue with household ammonia (or any other strong alkaline such as washing soda dissolved in a small amount of water) and dab it on the page. The writing instantly turns a purplish red.

Be careful not to *rub* the writing with the cotton because that will smear the letters. When the paper dries, the red letters vanish again.

3 · Inks That Glow in Blacklight

Many different substances will make invisible inks that shine in ultraviolet radiation or so-called "blacklight." Such inks are now widely used for stamping the back of your hand at skating rinks, dance halls, and amusement parks so you can be identified as having paid admission in case you want to leave and come back later. Banks are using blacklight for seeing otherwise invisible signatures on identification cards. Psychedelic posters with colors that glow in blacklight are currently popular.

The simplest way to make an ink that can be seen only in blacklight is to dissolve in water any type of household laundry detergent (avoid dishwashing detergents) containing a chemical for brightening clothes. These artificial whiteners become activated by the ultraviolet radiation in sunlight. Contrary to what you may have read elsewhere, solutions of flour, cooking starch, baking soda, or aspirin will not work—at least not with the kind of blacklight you will be using.

You and your friends must, of course, have a source of backlight. Fluorescent blacklight tubes, which fit fluorescent tube fixtures of standard sizes, can be bought at electrical supply stores or at many hardware stores.*

A word of caution. Shortwave ultraviolet radiation can damage the eyes and skin. Be certain to use only tubes that emit *longwave* ultraviolet radiation. The Edmund catalog has several pages of longwave blacklight tubes and accessories. If you buy a tube at a hardware store or electrical supply store, be sure to get the more expensive longwave tubes with filters to screen out the harmful shorter waves. Even with longwave filter tubes, you should wear dark sunglasses while using the radiation and avoid looking directly at the tube.

Testing will be necessary to determine which detergent works best and how much water to add. Too much water weakens the glow and too little

---

* You can order them by mail from the Edmund Scientific Company, 604 Edscorp Building, Barrington, New Jersey 08007. The company also sells bottles of invisible ink for use with such tubes.

water makes a paste than can be seen on the page. The kind of paper is important. Avoid all white paper, such as most typewriter paper, that itself shines in blacklight. Darker paper or pasteboard, with a hard surface, works best. Postcards and white file cards are ideal. Some onion-skin typewriter paper works well, but thin yellow paper is too absorbent.

After some experimenting, you should have little trouble mixing an excellent ink which is invisible in ordinary light, but under blacklight-shines, like luminous paint, with a milky white glow.

Because typewriter paper glows under ultraviolet radiation, a novel idea suggests itself. Is it possible to write on typewriter paper with a substance that does *not* glow, causing the writing to appear dark under blacklight? Unfortunately, the only substances I could find that worked well were also so opaque on the page that the writing could be seen easily in slanted light, or when the sheet was held in front of a strong light. This is the case, for instance, with chalk writing, or letters typed through the special white paper used for correcting typing errors. Writing done with water solutions of cooking starch and similar white substances is invisible when dry, but also fails to show as dark writing under ultraviolet radiation.

Perhaps you can discover a simple way to produce "black writing" which can be seen only when typewriter paper is shining under blacklight.

4 · Inks That Appear When Powdered

One of the best inks of this type is plain ordinary milk. Apply it with a brush on a thick, hard-surfaced paper or thin cardboard, such as a file card.

To bring out the writing, rub any kind of dark powdery substance over the dry page; cigarette ash, graphite, powdered charcoal, and so on. A good system is to scrape the point of a lead pencil, letting the powder fall on a sheet of paper. Tap your fingertips on the graphite powder, then rub them over the invisible writing.

5 · Writing That Becomes Visible When the Sheet Is Wet

There are many chemical formulas for sympathetic inks which are developed by wetting the sheet with water. Here is a valuable, little-known method of producing such writing without using any ink at all! Instead you use a watermark, which is an invisible mark made on paper by pressure printing. The pressure alters the fibers of the paper in such a way that the mark can be seen when the paper is wet, or, in some cases, when the sheet is held in front of a strong light. Watermarks are put on most postage stamps to make them harder to counterfeit and on quality paper to identify the manufacturer.

You can do your own watermark writing as follows. Dip a sheet of paper in water, then flatten it against a windowpane or large wall mirror. Place a dry sheet over it. Print your secret message on the dry sheet, using a ballpoint pen or a pencil with medium-hard lead and a point that is *not* sharp. Press hard while you write. When you finish the message, remove the dry sheet and destroy it. The printing will be clearly visible on the wet sheet.

When the sheet dries, the letters will vanish without a trace! Plunge the sheet into water. The writing immediately is visible again!

6 · Writing That Can Be Seen in Slanting Light

This method also uses pressure to alter the fibers of a sheet of paper. As before, a blank sheet goes on top of another, but in this case both sheets are dry. Print the message on the top sheet with a ballpoint pen or a hard lead pencil, applying firm pressure. Destroy the top sheet.

The writing on the other sheet is best seen by taking it into a dark room and shining a small fountain-pen-size flashlight on the page at the steepest possible angle. The lens of the flashlight should be right at the edge of the page. Photographers call this a "raking light" because it rakes over the page and shows up the slightest irregularities on the surface. If you don't have a small flashlight, paste a piece of black opaque paper, with a tiny hole in it, over the lens of a large flashlight.

This method of seeing faint impressions on a

sheet of paper (along with chemical and other methods) is often used in police and spy work. Sometimes when a message is written on the top sheet of a pad, and the sheet is removed, an impression will be left on the next page, or even on the next several pages, that can be read by raking the page with a narrow beam of light.

7 · Typing That Can Be Seen in Raking Light

Instead of a pen or pencil, a typewriter can be used to produce excellent pressure writing which is invisible until it is illuminated by a raking light. Simply put two sheets of blank paper in the typewriter and type your message. Destroy the sheet on which you typed. The impressions made by the keys on the second sheet will be impossible to see.

Take the blank sheet into a dark room and rake it with light held at the right edge of the paper. The typed letters will stand out clearly.

It's a good plan to type a false letter first, using an ordinary black typewriter ribbon and double spacing between the lines. Remove the sheet, put another sheet on top of it, reinsert both sheets in the typewriter, and type the secret message so that the impressions are between the lines of the false message.

If you prefer, you can do pressure typing directly on the page by moving the little lever that allows the typewriter keys to miss the ribbon. (This is how mimeograph stencils are cut too.) Be sure the keys are clean, and use a light touch so that the impressions can't be seen in ordinary light. The disadvantage of this method is that you can't see what you are typing, but it does make it easy to type invisible impressions between the lines of a false letter.

CHAPTER 7

Bizarre
Methods of
Message
Sending

It is impossible to describe all the weird methods spies have used to send secret messages. Many of them are not practical methods, such as shaving a girl's head, tattooing the message on her scalp, letting her hair grow back, then sending the girl. Or feeding a message to a cat, sending the cat, and killing the cat to obtain the message. Or writing on the shell of an egg with a solution of one ounce of alum to a pint of vinegar. The egg is hardboiled and sent. When its shell is removed, the writing is visible on the egg.

Just before World War II the Germans developed and used a photographic method of conveying secret information by microdots. An entire page of printing, or a diagram of a secret device, was photographed and the picture reduced to the size of a printed period. The method went undetected until 1941 when the F.B.I. pried such a period off a letter carried by a German spy and discovered that it was a photographic negative pasted on the page. By enlarging the picture, the hidden text was disclosed.

A remarkable method, developed in the United States in the mid-fifties, uses a flexible glass tube made up of hundreds of thousands of hair-thin strands of what is called "optical glass." Each strand transmits a tiny spot of light. If the fibers are woven together in a random way, the two ends of the tube will have different patterns. An image of printing that enters one end comes out the other end so jumbled that nothing is recognizable. By keeping the ends of a bundle of glass fibers fixed and twisting the center, it is possible to scramble the fibers in the same way on both halves of the resulting tube. When the tube is sliced in half, the sliced ends will have identical patterns. One half of the tube can be used to scramble the light and dark spots of a photograph so hopelessly that the only way to unscramble them is to view the picture through the other half of the tube.

The following methods may seem almost as strange, but they are simple and practical and you can actually use them.

I · The Dot Code

To operate this code you and your friends must

have duplicate strips of cardboard on which the
letters of the alphabet have been typed with even
spacing. For fast encoding the letters should be
in alphabetical order, but the code is harder to
break if the letters are scrambled. Type the random
letters on a sheet of paper, then cut out the line and
paste it on a narrow strip of cardboard. Leave
about an inch between the left end of the cardboard
and the first letter in the row:

H B F S T E Z K A J L G R C I Y U P D Q M V N X W O

Use lined notepaper for the secret dot message.
To encode the word APPLE, put the strip just below
the first horizontal line, its left edge flush with the
paper's left edge. Make a dot on the line directly
above the letter A. Move the strip down to the
next line, always keeping its left edge against the
left side of the sheet, and make a dot over P. In this
way the position of each dot symbolizes a letter.
If you use the strip pictured here, the word APPLE
will look like this:

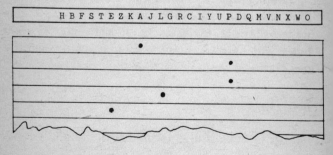

The dots are easily decoded by anyone who has a strip exactly like the one you used for encoding.

To disguise the importance of the dots, you can draw meaningless lines connecting the dots to make the page look like a map or diagram.

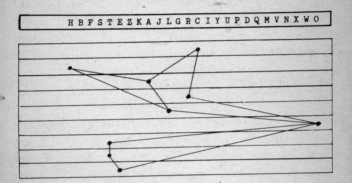

HBFSTEZKAJLGRCIYUPDQMVNXWO

This doesn't interfere in any way with decoding. Be careful, however, not to draw intersecting lines because the intersections might be wrongly assumed to be spots in the code. Can you read the word concealed in the above picture?

Another way to disguise the code is to make tiny pin holes in the paper instead of dots. Now you can write or type a fake message on the sheet. The pin holes will hardly be noticeable. Even if someone sees them, he won't know what they mean.

2 · The Knot Code

Instead of dots, use *knots!* Encoding and decoding is done with a cardboard or cloth strip like the one used for the dot code, but a much longer one because you need more space between each pair of letters.

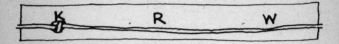

Have you already guessed how it works? Stretch a long piece of string along the strip, holding one end at the left end of the strip. Tie a knot at the spot that corresponds to the first letter of the message. Pull the knot tight. Now move the knot to the left end of the strip and tie a second knot at a spot that marks the second letter of the message. Continue in this way for the other letters. When you finish, you'll have a long piece of cord with tight little knots, scattered apparently at random. If your message is a long one, you will use a great deal of string. Send the string to your friend. Of course to decode the message, he'll need a strip exactly like yours.

Who would suspect that a long piece of knotted cord could conceal a message? It is an ancient method and one that has actually been used many times in the past.

3 · The Playing Card Code

In this unusual method a deck of ordinary playing cards carries the secret message. It should be a deck of bridge cards with pictures on the back so that all 52 cards can be arranged with the pictures turned the same way. In addition, the cards are also arranged in an order on which you and your friends have agreed. For example, from the top down, the ace to king of spades, followed by hearts, clubs, and diamonds, each suit in the same ace-to-king order.

After the cards are in proper sequence, square them neatly and hold them together tightly with one hand. Print the message with a pencil around the deck's four edges. Use capital letters, slanting all vertical and horizontal lines in one direction as shown.

Turn half the deck around, so that the backs of the two halves go in opposite directions, and shuffle the two halves together. Shuffle several more times. The message will be completely obliterated. It is really a kind of transposition code, but one that mixes up bits of each letter in much the same way as the glass-fiber-tube method described at the beginning of this chapter. Slanting vertical and horizontal lines of the letters makes the scrambling more effective.

The person who receives the deck arranges the cards in the agreed-upon order, with the picture sides turned in the same direction. Then he reads the printing around the deck's edges. He can now erase the pencil marks and use the same deck to send back a reply.

4 · The Red-Blue Code

Many stationery stores sell red cellophane wrapping paper. It can be used for the instant decoding of secret messages, maps, diagrams or anything you want to write or draw on a sheet of paper.

First write a phony message, or draw a fake picture, using a red pencil. The secret message is then put on the same sheet with a blue pencil sharpened to a fine point. Write as lightly as you can, so that only a very faint blue line is made. It will be almost impossible to see because of the heavy red lines. Be sure to do the blue writing directly on top of the red lines rather than at empty places on the page.

To see the blue writing, put the red cellophane on top of the page. The red lines disappear like magic, while the faint blue lines stand out sharp and clear.

5 · The Crayon Cover

Write the secret message lightly with a pencil

because you want the letters to be as faint as possible. Obliterate the message completely by rubbing colored crayons over it. To disguise what you have done, use several colors to make a picture of some sort, perhaps a landscape with blue sky and green grass. Be sure that every letter is completely covered by a color.

To read the message, the receiver scrapes away the crayon colors with the edge of a sharp knife. There it is!

6 · The Crease Code

Fold a sheet of typewriter paper three times, as shown in the illustration. Open it up and print the letters of your message vertically along the two vertical creases:

Add null letters on both sides of these letters to make dummy words. Try to think of words that will make the page read like a letter saying something that has no relation to the secret message. For example:

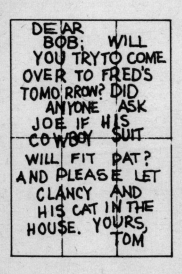

To read the concealed message, the receiver has only to run his eyes down the vertical creases. It is a ridiculously simple form of secret writing, but it has one great merit. It can be decoded very quickly.

You can get a much longer message on one page by writing words along the creases instead of letters. In this variation dummy words should be written between the "crease words" to make it look like an ordinary letter. On page 99, the sheet is folded to make three vertical creases instead of two.

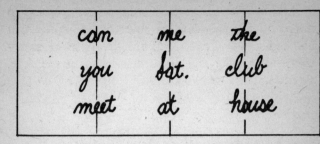

can	me	the
you	Sat.	club
meet	at	house

you can let me see the pics
of you next Sat. the club will
not meet Mon. at Joe's house Bill

7 · The Swizzle Stick Code

Transparent plastic or glass stirring rods, sometimes called "swizzle sticks," can be bought in any dime store. They are used for mixing drinks. Hold such a rod horizontally over a line of print, close to the page but not touching it, and look at the letter through the solid glass or plastic. You will see a strange thing. The rod acts as a cylindrical lens, turning each letter upside down and simultaneously creating a mirror image. This is the basis of a whimsical cipher which I myself invented many years ago.

The secret message is written by using the substitution cipher alphabet shown below. A cipher text will look like this:

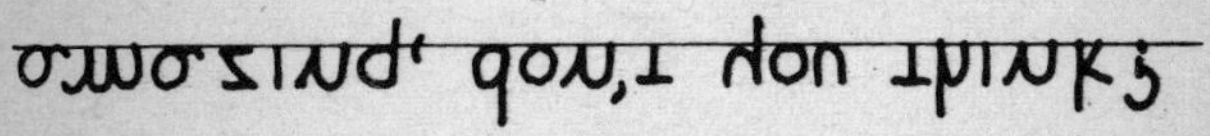

ᴄꜱᴡᴏᴢɪɴ� don't don ɪᴘɪɴꜱꜱꜱ

The message is decoded instantly, merely by reading it through a swizzle stick! If you have a transparent stirring rod in the house, try it and see how magically the rod translates the cipher.

If a stirring rod is not available, there are two other ways to decode this cipher. One is to turn the page upside down and hold it up to a mirror. The other way—if the cipher is written on thin paper—is to turn the paper over, turn the printing upside down, and hold the sheet up to a strong light so that you can read the printing *through* the paper.

Note the light horizontal lines above the cipher symbols, on the alphabet key and on the sample cipher message. It is a good plan to rule these lines lightly with a pencil before you write a coded message. They will help you place the symbols in their proper spots so that the printing will look right when you decode it.

A	B	C	D	E	F	G	H	I

J	K	L	M	N	O	P	Q	R

S	T	U	V	W	X	Y	Z	?

CHAPTER 8

Codes for
Other
Worlds

All the codes so far considered are intended to make messages *difficult* for anyone who knows English to read unless he knows the method of decoding. In this chapter we consider a problem that is almost the opposite. How can one send a message that is as *easy* to read as possible, and by someone who *doesn't* know our language? Indeed, the receiver of the message may not even be an earth person!

This is a problem in communication which is now being studied intensively by many astronomers, mathematicians, and language experts. It has to do with sending messages to, or receiving them from, other planets on which there may be intelligent life.

Astronomers now believe it is extremely unlikely

that there is intelligent life on any other planet in our own solar system. Earlier in this century, long before our space probes began taking close-up photographs of Mars, many astronomers were convinced that Mars was inhabited by intelligent creatures. Perhaps you have read some of the novels about Martians by Edgar Rice Burroughs, or *The War of the Worlds* by H. G. Wells, which was the basis for Orson Welles's famous radio broadcast describing a fictional invasion of the earth by Martians.

In days when the existence of Martians seemed a real possibility, many scientists pondered the question: How could we send a message to Mars that would let the Martians know we exist? One plan was to build an enormous searchlight for

THE PYTHAGOREAN THEOREM

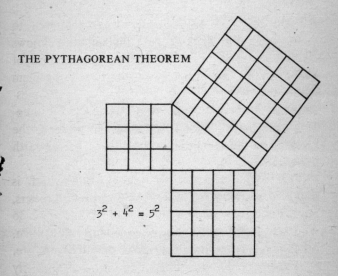

$$3^2 + 4^2 = 5^2$$

blinking code messages, which could be picked up by Martian telescopes. Another plan was to construct long chains of huge lights which would form a picture of a simple geometric figure, such as a square or a circle, or perhaps diagram a basic theorem of geometry.

The Pythagorean theorem, for instance, states that the square of the hypotenuse of a right triangle is equal in area to the sum of the squares of the other two sides. It is so important in plane geometry that if the Martians knew geometry and saw in their telescopes a diagram such as the one shown on the previous page, they would recognize its meaning at once.

Astronomers today no longer believe that there are Martians, Venusians, Jovians, or Saturnians. What about intelligent life on planets that go around other suns in our Milky Way galaxy? Is anyone out there? No one knows for sure, but most astronomers think the answer is yes. If intelligent beings *are* there, perhaps they have been trying for centuries to communicate with other planets by radio code. In 1960 one of our large radio telescopes, at Green Bank, West Virginia, began scanning the sky for such messages. The project was named Project Ozma after the girl ruler of the Land of Oz. No messages were detected and the project was abandoned, but the listening is still going on with other radio telescopes here and in other countries, including the Soviet Union.

If we received from outer space a series of radio-wave beeps, how would we know that it came from intelligent creatures; that it was not just radio "noise," which had some natural cause? In other words, if were tried to reach life on another planet by radio-code beeps, how could we best attract the attention of our listeners so they would know at once that someone was trying to talk to them?

The simplest way would be to send whole numbers in counting order, 1, 2, 3, 4, 5. . . . First a single beep, then beep-beep, then beep-beep-beep, and so on. It is hard to imagine that such a series of beeps would be caused by anything except intelligent minds capable of counting. And counting numbers are the same on any planet. If inhabitants of a distant planet—let's call it Planet Zeta—counted the stars or pebbles or other creatures like themselves, or anything at all that came in distinct units, they would count exactly the same way we do. Of course they might use a different base system for symbolizing their numbers. If they had twelve fingers instead of ten, they would probably prefer a 12-based system to a 10-based one. But when counting numbers are sent by a series of beeps, it doesn't matter what base system is used to record them.

Once we had attracted the attention of the Zetans by a series of counting numbers, we could start teaching them the beep signals we were using for addition, subtraction, multiplication, division, and equal. For instance, we send beep-beep, pause, a beep signal meaning "plus," pause, three more beeps, pause, a signal meaning "equals," pause, then five beeps. Because the Zetans already know that two plus three is five, they would guess that the second signal meant "plus" and the fourth signal meant "equals." In similar fashion we could teach the Zetans our signals for the other arithmetic operations. Zero is important. We could communicate our signal for it by sending such equations as $8 + 0 = 8, 0 + 7 = 7, 5 \times 0 = 0, 0 + 0 = 0$, and so on.

Now comes the most crucial step of all. We send, over and over again, an equation such as $31 \times 41 = 1,271$ (after teaching a place-value notation so that we can transmit 1,271 without having to send 1,271 beeps!). Then we send a string of exactly 1,271 digits consisting only of zeros and ones, apparently in a random order. This series of 1,271 digits would be repeated many times. Perhaps the Zetans would record it and play it over as often as they wished, so they could study it carefully. What does the series mean?

Well, if listeners are smart enough to have built instruments capable of receiving radio signals from a distant planet, they probably are smart enough to know how to produce pictures by scanning a rectangular matrix of cells, using 1 to indicate a cell that is black and 0 to indicate a cell that remains empty. True, they might not see the world the same way we do, and what we call "black" may not apply to their senses. But it doesn't matter. All that matters is that they distinguish 1-cells from 0-cells.

This is the technique by which newspaper pictures are sent by radio, the technique by which pictures appear on a television screen, and by which pictures of the Moon and Mars are radioed back to earth from our spaceprobe cameras. It is such a simple and obvious technique that surely Zeta's scientists would know about it.

Have you guessed, now what the number 1,271 means? It has two prime factors: 31 and 41. Prime numbers can be evenly divided only by themselves and by 1, so in this case, 31 and 41 are the only factors (divisors) of 1,271. The two factors suggest a matrix that is 31 by 41 cells. It is the only rectangular matrix that can have exactly 1,271 cells.

The Zetans would not, of course, know what scanning path we were using. Is it left to right by rows, or right to left? Is it up and down by columns? Does the path weave back and forth like a plow? Could it be a spiral? Zetan cryptographers would try the simplest paths first, just as a cryptanalyst on earth tries simple paths when he attempts to crack a transposition cipher based on matrix paths (see Chapter 1). The first picture we send by scanning should be something uncomplicated and fundamental, like a triangle or circle. As soon as the Zetans found a scanning path that produced such a picture, they would know immediately the method of scanning we were using.

From now on, all sorts of pictures could be sent to convey more complicated information. Alongside each picture we would transmit the picture of our word for that picture. Eventually we could go on to animated drawings or even motion pictures to communicate still more complicated ideas.

The illustration below was drawn by Bernard M. Oliver, and is reproduced from his article in the anthology, *Interstellar Communication,* edited by A. G. W. Cameron. It represents a picture obtained by scanning a 31-by-41 matrix of 1,271 cells (it was because of this picture that I used a matrix of that size as an example) with a series of 1,271 digits made up of zeros and ones. Oliver gives the entire series in his article. It begins: 1000000 . . . Scanning the rows from left to right, and taking rows from top to bottom as in ordinary reading, the

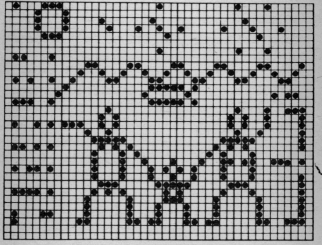

A PICTURE WE COULD RECEIVE IN CODE
FROM ANOTHER PLANET

seven digits indicate that in the first row a spot goes in the first cell and the next six cells are empty. The picture is one which we might receive from outer space, perhaps from Mars. Oliver explains his picture as follows:

"Apparently we are in touch with a race of erect bipeds who reproduce sexually. There is even a suggestion that they might be mammals. The crude circle and column of dots at the left suggests their sun and planetary system. The figure is pointing to the fourth planet, evidently their home. The planets are numbered down the left-hand edge in a binary code which increases in place value from left to right and starts with a decimal (or rather a binary) point to mark the beginning. The wavy line commencing at the third planet indicates that it is covered with water and the fishlike form shows there is marine life there. The bipeds know this, so they must have space travel. The diagrams at the top will be recognized as hydrogen, carbon, and oxygen atoms, so their life is based on a carbohydrate chemistry. The binary number six above the raised arm of the right figure suggests six fingers and implies a base-twelve number system. Finally, the dimension line at the lower right suggests that the figure is eleven somethings tall. Since the wavelength of 21 cm on which we received the message is the only length we both know, we conclude the beings are 231 cm, or seven feet, in height."

Unfortunately, we can't talk back and forth with Zetans the way we talk to one another by telephone here on earth. The stars are much too far away. The nearest star system—Alpha Centauri and its companion stars—is a little more than four light years away. This means that, if Zeta circled one of the suns in this nearby system, we would have to wait almost nine years before we could expect to receive an answer. (Radio waves travel at the speed of light.) However, in those nine years both we and Zetans could send each other vast amounts of coded information.

We have no way of knowing in advance whether Zetans would be friendly toward us or hostile. They could be so far ahead of us in intelligence and technology that once they knew we were here they might dispatch a spaceship to collect some human specimens for their laboratories and zoos.

Not long ago someone asked the famous Chinese physicist Chen Ning Yang what we should do if we ever received an unmistakable radio message from outer space. His reply was:

"Don't answer."

References for
Further
Reading

Historical

DAVID KAHN, *The Codebreakers* (Macmillan, 1967). This 1,164-page work is the most accurate, most complete history of cryptography ever written.

FLETCHER PRATT, *Secret and Urgent* (Bobbs-Merrill, 1939; Doubleday, 1941). The best earlier attempt at a general history.

DAN TYLER MOORE and MARTHA WALLER, *Cloak and Cipher* (Bobbs-Merrill, 1962). Another popularly written history.

MAJOR HERBERT OSBORNE YARDLEY, *The American Black Chamber* (Bobbs-Merrill, 1931). The sensational story of American cryptography from 1919 to 1928, by the nation's most famous, most colorful cryptanalyst.

BARBARA W. TUCHMAN, *The Zimmermann Telegram* (Viking, 1958). The story of the famous German cablegram of World War I and how its code was broken by British intelligence.

LADISLAS FARAGO, *The Broken Seal* (Random House, 1967). Covers twenty years of spying and codebreaking by the United States and Japan, including our cracking of the Japanese machine code of World War II.

Methods

JAMES RAYMOND WOLFE, *Secret Writing* (McGraw-Hill, 1970).

JOHN LAFFIN, *Codes and Ciphers* (Abelard-Schumann, 1964).

LAURENCE DWIGHT SMITH, *Cryptography* (Norton, 1943; Dover paperback, 1955).

ALEXANDER D'AGAPEYEFF, *Codes and Ciphers* (Oxford University Press, 1932).

ANDRÉ LANGIE, *Cryptography,* translated from the French by J. C. H. Macbeth (Constable & Co., London, 1922).

HENRY LYSING (pseudonym of John Leonard Nanovic), *Secret Writing* (David Kemp, 1936). A book for children, based on the author's department which appeared regularly in *The Shadow Magazine*.

WILLIAM F. FRIEDMAN, "Cryptology," *The Encyclopaedia Britannica,* all editions since 1929. A classic article by the world's greatest cryptanalyst.

DAVID KAHN, "Cryptology," *The Encyclopedia Americana* (1970).

Codebreaking

HELEN FOUCHÉ GAINES, *Cryptanalysis* (Dover, 1956). A paperback reprint of a 1939 book, but still the best book available on the art of cipher breaking.

ABRAHAM SINKOV, *Elementary Cryptanalysis* (Random House paperback, 1968).

DONALD MILLIKIN, *Elementary Cryptography* (New York University Bookstore, 1943).

JACK M. WOLFE, *A First Course in Cryptanalysis* (Brooklyn College Press, 1943).

Cipher Cranks

WILLIAM F. FRIEDMAN and ELIZABETH S. FRIEDMAN, *The Shakespearean Ciphers Examined* (Cambridge University Press, 1957). The definitive study of misguided efforts to discover hidden messages in Shakespeare's plays.

Interplanetary Communication

I. S. SHKLOVSKII and CARL SAGAN, *Intelligent Life in the Universe* (Holden-Day, 1966; Dell paperback, 1971).

WALTER SULLIVAN, *We Are Not Alone* (McGraw-Hill, 1964; Signet paperback, 1969).

ALISTAIR G. W. CAMERON, *Interstellar Communication* (W. A. Benjamin, 1963).

MARTIN GARDNER, "Extraterrestrial Communication," Chapter 25 in *Martin Gardner's Sixth Book of Mathematical Games from Scientific American* (W. H. Freeman, 1971).

29549 SPACE PUZZLES: *Curious Questions and Answers About the Solar System,* by Martin Gardner. Illustrated with photographs, diagrams, and drawings. Test your knowledge about the frontiers of space as you sharpen your wits on these intriguing puzzles of our solar system. (75¢)

29309 DANNY DUNN *and the Smallifying Machine,* by Jay Williams and Raymond Abrashkin. Illustrated by Paul Sagsoorian. When Danny gets trapped in Professor Bullfinch's latest invention, he shrinks to insect size and must face survival in a world that has become a giant jungle. (60¢)

29566 WHITE WATER, STILL WATER, by J. Allan Bosworth. Illustrated by Charles W. Walker. Swept down river on a raft, Chris faces a hazardous journey home through the wilderness—barefoot and equipped with nothing but a broken-bladed pocketknife. (75¢)

29567 TODAY I AM A HAM, by Ethelyn M. Parkinson. Illustrated by Ralph J. McDonald. When Eric decides to become a ham radio operator, he has a hilarious and madcap time trying to solve such problems as no equipment, no money, and no job. (75¢)

(If your bookseller does not have the titles you want, you may order them by sending the retail price, plus 25¢ for postage and handling to: Mail Service Department, POCKET BOOKS, a division of Simon & Schuster, Inc., 1 West 39th Street, New York, N. Y. 10018. Please enclose check or money order—do not send cash.)